REAL STORIES

BOOK 1

NEW YORK, June 17.—A fireman rescued a 76-year-old woman from a burning apartment building yesterday by tossing her off a fire escape. The woman, Mrs. Mary Rogers, landed safely in the arms of another fireman waiting on the roof of an adjoining building.

Fireman Edward Lane had risked his life to reach the woman, who was trapped in her smoke-filled top floor apartment in the five-story building. The fire was blazing out of control as Lane carried the almost unconscious woman onto a fire escape.

As flames threatened them, Lane tried without success to first climb to the roof and then to go below the height of the flames. He could not do so while carrying the dead-weight of the helpless 115-pound woman.

Then he saw another fireman, Mike Mays, motioning to him with his arms held out. Mays was on the roof of the next building, which was level with the fire escape. A space of only four feet separated the two buildings, but there was a fifty-foot drop to the ground. Lane tried to pass Mrs. Rogers over to Mays, but the gap was too wide.

Then the two men decided that the only chance to save the woman was to try something very dangerous. Lane reached back and threw Mrs.

NERVOUS MINUTES

Are there times when a child should not obey his parents?

Priscilla Browo is a very

Success comes fro a combination of luck, natural abilit and hard work.

When Roland Kirk was teen years old, he drea one night he was playing t musical instruments — all the same time. He made dream come true. Today h a brilliant musician with a ent so real few people can lieve it.

When he blows one h (for example, the tenor sa phone), he is the equal of a musician around today. W he blows three horns at same time, he is truly out this world.

Kirk is a one-man band, master of forty-five mus

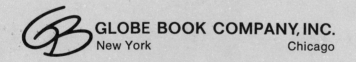

GLOBE BOOK COMPANY, INC.
New York   Chicago

real stories
book 1

Milton Katz

Michael Chakeres
Murray Bromberg

Second Edition 1975

ISBN: 0-87065-204-4

This edition may be used with all
other editions, in the same classroom,
without conflict of any kind.

Illustrations by Harry J. Schaare
Cover design by Lawrence Schaeffer
Text design by Edward Zytko

MANUFACTURED IN THE UNITED STATES OF AMERICA

20   19   18   17   16   15   14   13   12   11

ABOUT THE AUTHORS

MILTON KATZ, the chairman of English at Thomas Jefferson High School, Brooklyn, N.Y., has been a program writer for the Responsive Environment Center. He is the editor of *Moonlight Review,* a national teachers' literary magazine. Mr. Katz holds the degrees of B.A. from Brooklyn College and M.A. from New York University.

MICHAEL CHAKERES, an expert in the field of reading and reading curriculum development, is presently a teacher of English at Susan E. Wagner High School, Staten Island, New York. He holds a Secondary School Principal's license from New York State and has been laboratory supervisor and coordinator of the Responsive Environment Program. Mr. Chakeres holds the degree of B.A. from Brooklyn College.

MURRAY BROMBERG has taught English and been Chairman of English at Thomas Jefferson High School, Brooklyn, New York. Mr. Bromberg has also taught at Hofstra University. Now principal of Andrew Jackson High School, Queens, New York, he is the author of several books including *Our American Language, Making Literature Lessons Live, Getting Your Students To Write More Effectively, One Hundred Great Scientists* and has compiled two anthologies, *World-Wide Essays* and *Literature of Mystery: Four Representative Types.*

He has published articles in *Shakespeare Quarterly* and other periodicals. Mr. Bromberg holds the degrees of B.A. from Brooklyn College and M.A. from Columbia University.

ACKNOWLEDGMENTS

For permission to reprint copyrighted materials, grateful acknowledgment is made to the following publishers and news services:

"Is King a Killer . . . ?" reprinted with permission of *The Chattanooga News-Free Press* and The Associated Press.

"The Fall from the Sixth-Floor Window," copyright © 1959 by the New York Times Company. Reprinted with permission.

"Surprise!" reprinted with permission of the United Press International.

"Flying Saucer" reprinted with permission from the *Chicago Sun-Times* and United Press International.

"The Turtle with Two Heads," copyright © 1966 by the New York Times Company. Reprinted with permission.

"Giggling Auto Mechanics" reprinted with permission of the United Press International.

"A Machine to Make the Beds" reprinted with permission of Reuters News Service.

"Raining Frogs" reprinted from *Newsday*, Long Island. Copyright © 1966, Newsday, Inc.

"Quick Thinking" reprinted with permission of the United Press International.

"A Mystery," copyright © 1959 by the New York Times Company. Reprinted by permission.

"A Housewife's Easy Day" reprinted with permission of the Canadian Press.

"The Man Who Wouldn't Sleep," copyright © 1959 by the New York Times Company. Reprinted with permission.

"The Artist Was a Truant" reprinted with permission of *Ebony*.

viii

CONTENTS

INTRODUCTION

Welcome to REAL STORIES! We think that is a good name for this book because each story is a *real* one. The stories are taken from real life and adapted from the newspapers or magazines in which they first appeared.

There are many different kinds of stories, yet each one has a special interest. Some are funny, and some are serious; some will make you think, but some will surprise you. There are stories about people, animals and even about machines. Some people in these stories are white and some are black, some are young and some old. In other words, you will find a mixture in REAL STORIES that you find in life.

Although the reports of real-life happenings will hold your interest, they will do more than that. They will help you to become a better reader. To do so, you will have to understand what you read, and you will have to know the meanings of some new words. Each selection in REAL STORIES teaches you how to learn new words and how to make better use of words you already know. In addition, you are invited to express yourself 'in writing or in class discussion on lively topics.

Ahead of you are worthwhile hours with stories of flying saucers, mechanical housemaids, ghosts, exciting rescues, detective work and witch doctors. We know that your enjoyment of REAL STORIES will be real.

1

1. IS KING A KILLER OR ... ¿ES UN PERRO AFABLE?

WERE YOU EVER FRIGHTENED BY AN ANGRY DOG? WHY WAS THE DOG MEAN TO YOU?

WHAT CLUES DOES THIS STORY GIVE YOU ABOUT LEARNING TO GET ALONG BETTER WITH ANIMALS—OR EVEN WITH PEOPLE?

King is a watchdog at an Air Force *base* in Tennessee. At one point, King was about to be *destroyed*. The Air Force said he was too mean to train. He was *vicious*. They said, "He hates everybody, everything that moves and everything touching him."

But King was not so tough after all. The Air Force *discovered* that King had been *raised* by a Spanish-speaking family before he was sold to the Air Force. All that King wanted was someone to give him his orders in Spanish. Spanish was the only language he knew.

King was given a new trainer who speaks Spanish. Now King is happy and the Air Force is happy with him.

— CHATTANOOGA NEWS-FREE PRESS

3

1. Another title that would best explain the main idea of this story is:
   (a) The Air Force
   (b) King, a Changed Watchdog
   (c) Speaking Spanish to Dogs
   (d) How to Train a Dog
2. King was
   (a) destroyed.
   (b) a watchdog.
   (c) always easy to get along with.
   (d) raised by an English-speaking family.
3. King hated everybody because
   (a) he was trained that way.
   (b) he did not understand his orders.
   (c) he was treated badly by his trainers.
   (d) he was a watchdog.
4. The Air Force did not destroy King because
   (a) he became happy when his orders were given in Spanish.
   (b) he had been raised by a Spanish-speaking family.
   (c) the Air Force needed him as a watchdog.
   (d) he was vicious.

REACHING OUT

¿Es Un Perro Afable? In the title of this story is a Spanish sentence that means:
   (a) Is Spanish Better than English?
   (b) Is He a Friendly Dog?

4

(c) Is the Air Force Kind?
(d) Is the Sergeant Spanish?

FIRST THINGS FIRST

Arrange these events in the order in which they happened.

1. King was given a new trainer.
2. King was about to be destroyed.
3. The Air Force found out that King had been raised by a Spanish-speaking family.
4. King was happy.
5. King was a vicious watchdog.

IMPROVING YOUR VOCABULARY

In the first column below and on the next page are the five words in italics from the story. Pick out the best "story" meaning of these words.

1. an army *base* — (a) a place where games are played; (b) a place where soldiers stay; (c) a place where dogs are kept

2. to be *destroyed* — (a) killed; (b) loved; (c) found

3. a *vicious* dog — (a) friendly; (b) mean; (c) lost

4. *discovered* the dog — (a) beat; (b) gave away; (c) found out for the first time

5. *raised* by a family   (a) brought up; (b) taken away; (c) brought in

---

WORD BUILDING

The word *trainer* in the story above means *a person who trains, or teaches.* When you see *er* or *or* at the end of a word, it will almost always mean *a person who.*

Example: *baker* means *a person who bakes*

To Do: Write the meaning of each of these words in your notebook. Use the form of the word that is in the parentheses.

    1. worker (works)
    2. catcher (catches)
    3. mover (moves)
    4. killer (kills)
    5. speaker (speaks)

EXPRESSING YOURSELF

1. When a person does something wrong, it is some-
    times better to try to understand, rather than
    punish him. When do you think understanding
    would be more helpful than punishing someone?
2. Tell how you can train an animal to obey orders
    or to do tricks.
3. Why do people sometimes do wrong things
    when they do not understand others, and others
    do not understand them?
4. Some people are "loners"—they have no friends.

6

Why? Can someone who has no friends at all be happy?

5. Write a paragraph about a young person you know who had trouble making friends. What would you tell him to do so he could get along better with people?

2. THE FALL FROM THE SIXTH-FLOOR WINDOW

WHAT IS AN "ACCIDENT"? WHY DO ACCIDENTS HAPPEN? CAN THE WAY YOU FEEL AT THE TIME HELP CAUSE AN ACCIDENT?

DID THE SCOLDING FROM HIS FATHER HAVE ANYTHING TO DO WITH JIMMY ROGERS' FALL?

A 13-year-old boy fell from a sixth-floor window, but he landed on a soft *patch* in the back yard and was not *seriously* hurt.

The police said that Jimmy had been scolded by his father because of poor school grades. Shortly after, the boy lost his *balance* and fell from the apartment window.

Jimmy's brother tried to stop him from falling but could not hold onto his wrists. Doctors at City Hospital said that Jimmy *fractured* his right ankle and hip when he landed in the dirt.

— NEW YORK TIMES

CHECK YOUR UNDERSTANDING

1. Another title that would best explain the main idea of this story is:
   (a) A Failing Student
   (b) An Angry Father
   (c) A Lucky Boy
   (d) In the Hospital
2. Jimmy was not killed because
   (a) his brother stopped his fall.
   (b) he landed in a soft spot of dirt.
   (c) he knew how to fall without getting hurt.
   (d) the doctors saved his life.
3. Jimmy fell because
   (a) he lost his balance.
   (b) he wanted to kill himself.
   (c) his brother pushed him.
   (d) he landed in a soft patch of the back yard.
4. Jimmy's brother couldn't stop the fall because
   (a) he didn't want to.
   (b) he didn't see Jimmy fall.

9

(c) Jimmy wouldn't let him.
(d) he couldn't hold onto Jimmy's wrists.
5. Jimmy
  (a) broke his arm.
  (b) was not hurt at all.
  (c) fractured his ankle and hip.
  (d) was killed.

FIRST THINGS FIRST

Arrange these events in the order in which they happened.

1. Jimmy's brother couldn't hold onto him.
2. Jimmy fractured his ankle and hip.
3. Jimmy's father scolded him.
4. Jimmy landed in a soft patch of the back yard.
5. Jimmy got poor grades in school.
6. Jimmy lost his balance and fell.

IMPROVING YOUR VOCABULARY

In the first column below and on the next page are the five words in italics from the story. Pick out the best "story" meaning of each of these words.

1. soft *patch*   (a) pool of water; (b) group of people; (c) piece of ground

2. not *seriously* hurt   (a) dangerously; (b) foolishly; (c) carelessly

10

3. *scolded* by his father   (a) praised; (b) found fault with; (c) beaten

4. lost his *balance*   (a) condition of not falling over; (b) school books; (c) coat and hat

5. *fractured* his ankle   (a) broke; (b) hurt; (c) covered

WORD BUILDING

The word *unable* in the story above means *not able. Un* is a prefix, or a part that is joined at the beginning of a word. The prefix *un* at the beginning of a word will almost always mean *not.*

To Do: In your notebook, write the meaning of each of these words that begin with *un*. The first one is done for you.

    1. unhappy—not happy
    2. unhurt
    3. unfriendly
    4. unkind
    5. unknown

A Little Harder: Match the meaning in column B to the proper *un* word in column A.

A	B
1. *unafraid* of trouble	(a) not right or just
2. *uninjured* by the fall	(b) without fear
3. *unemployed* after graduation	(c) different from
4. *unfair* to workers	(d) not hurt
5. *unlike* his brother	(e) not working

11

EXPRESSING YOURSELF

1. Did the scolding Jimmy's father gave him have anything to do with his fall?
2. Tell about an accident that happened to someone you know that would not have happened if the person had been more careful.
3. What should you do if there has been an accident and someone is hurt, but you cannot get help quickly?
4. Write a paragraph about a "close call" you have had.

WHAT WAS THE BIGGEST SURPRISE YOU EVER HAD?

HOW DOES YOUR SURPRISE COMPARE WITH
THE SURPRISE RECEIVED BY THE MAN
IN THIS STORY WHO WENT OUT
ONLY TO BUY SOME ICE?

BROOKVILLE, Ind., July 5 — A vending machine is a machine that sells *items* like candy, gum, soda, tissues and coffee. Some vending machines also sell ice.

Yesterday a *customer* walked up to a large ice-vending machine and dropped in his money. Instead of ice, he *received* quite a *surprise*.

The door opened and out came an arm. It was *attached* to Robert Morgan, the man who *fills* the machine with ice. Mr. Morgan was putting ice in the machine when the door *slammed* shut. No one was around to hear him call until the customer came and *released* him.

— INDIANAPOLIS STAR

CHECK YOUR UNDERSTANDING

1. Another title that would best explain the main idea of this story is:
   (a) A Shut Door
   (b) A Useless Call
   (c) The Ice Machine
   (d) Ice Machine Brings Surprise
2. The customer in this story went to the vending machine for
   (a) candy.
   (b) a surprise.
   (c) ice.
   (d) Mr. Morgan.
3. Robert Morgan was inside the machine because
   (a) the door had slammed shut behind him.
   (b) he was repairing it.
   (c) he wanted to surprise customers.
   (d) he was getting some ice.
4. The word *it* in the third paragraph means
   (a) Robert Morgan.
   (b) the door.
   (c) Robert Morgan's arm.
   (d) the machine.

5. Of the following items, a vending machine would most likely sell
  (a) automobiles.
  (b) cups and saucers.
  (c) shoes.
  (d) cigarettes.

FIRST THINGS FIRST

Arrange these events in the order in which they happened.

6 **1.** The customer let Mr. Morgan out.
4 **2.** The customer put his money in the machine.
1 **3.** Mr. Morgan filled the machine with ice.
5 **4.** The door opened and an arm came out.
2 **5.** The door slammed shut behind Mr. Morgan.
3 **6.** Mr. Morgan called, but no one heard him.

IMPROVING YOUR VOCABULARY

In the first column below and on the next page are the eight words in italics from the story. Pick out the best "story" meaning of each of these words.

1. many *items*   (a) people; (b) places; (c) things

2. *customer* came in   (a) person who sells; (b)
    C   repair man; (c) person who buys

3. *received* a gift   (a) gave; (b) got; (c)
    B   bought

15

4. got a *surprise*
A

(a) something not expected; (b) something that brings happiness; (c) something that is painful

5. an arm *attached*
C

(a) struck; (b) raised; (c) joined

6. *fills* the machine
B

(a) takes out from; (b) puts in as much as possible; (c) sharpens

7. door *slammed* shut
B

(a) hit with force; (b) closed with force; (c) was closed

8. *released* him
A

(a) let out; (b) was annoyed with; (c) spoke to

WORD BUILDING

The word *opened* in the story above is the past tense of *open*. When you see *ed* at the end of a word, it means that the action described by the word happened in the past.

Example: I *cook* the meal *now*.

Cook is happening in the present, right *now*.

Add *ed* to *cook*.

I *cooked* the meal *yesterday*.

The *ed* makes the cooking happen in the past.

To Do: There are six words in the story, besides *opened,* that end in *ed.*

Find each of these six words and list them in your notebook. Then write the present tense form

16

next to each word. The first one is done for you below.

PAST   PRESENT
1. walked   walk

A Little Harder: Write the past tense of each of these words: (Hint: When the present tense already ends in *e*, just add *d*.)

1. talk   **2.** play   **3.** listen   **4.** close   **5.** rest

---

EXPRESSING YOURSELF

1. Write a paragraph telling about a surprising thing that happened to you.
2. Have you ever had trouble working a machine such as a vending machine, a telephone or an automatic pinsetter in a bowling alley? What happened?
3. Imagine you are Mr. Morgan stuck inside the machine. Tell what his thoughts might have been.

4. FLYING SAUCER

WHAT IS A "FLYING SAUCER"? ARE THERE REALLY ANY SUCH THINGS?

MAYBE THIS STORY WILL HELP YOU DECIDE.

GALESBURG, Ill. (UPI) — Many people say they have seen flying saucers, but no saucer has ever been *captured*.

However, a "flying saucer" was brought in here in Galesburg.

A number of persons in the *area reported* seeing a *strange* flying *object*. *Finally,* guards at a Galesburg *factory* saw it and *hauled* it in.

They found that the "saucer" was really a kite with a light. On the red, plastic kite were two penlight batteries and a small bulb. Flying around in the night sky, the glowing kite looked to some people like a strange thing from outer space.

— CHICAGO SUN-TIMES

CHECK YOUR UNDERSTANDING

1. Another title that would best explain the main idea of this story is:
   (a) A Real Flying Saucer
   (b) The Flying Saucer That Was Really a Kite
   (c) The Guards at the Factory
   (d) A Kite with a Light
2. The "flying saucer" in Galesburg was really
   (a) from outer space.
   (b) never brought in.
   (c) a kite with a light.
   (d) the first real flying saucer ever captured.
3. The "flying saucer" in Galesburg was captured by
   (a) guards in a factory.
   (b) a number of people.
   (c) penlight batteries.
   (d) people from outer space.
4. The kite was *not*
   (a) a flying saucer.
   (b) made of plastic.
   (c) red in color.
   (d) glowing.

REACHING OUT

From reading this story, we can best say that:
(a) there are no such things as flying saucers.
(b) sometimes people think they see flying saucers, but they are really seeing something else.
(c) kites are always mistaken for flying saucers.
(d) flying saucers are often captured.

FIRST THINGS FIRST

Arrange these events in the order in which they happened.

1. Guards at a factory brought the "flying saucer" in.
2. People reported seeing a strange flying object.
3. A kite with a light was flying around at night.
4. It was found that the "flying saucer" was really a kite.

IMPROVING YOUR VOCABULARY

In the first column below and on the next page are the eight words in italics from the story. Pick out the best "story" meaning of each of these words.

1. none was *captured*   (a) taken prisoner; (b) seen; (c) returned

2. in the *area*   (a) flying object; (b) automobile; (c) neighborhood

3. people *reported*   (a) were afraid; (b) tried; (c) told

4. *strange* thing   (a) not seen before; (b) interesting; (c) strong

5. flying *object*   (a) thing; (b) bird; (c) plane

6. *finally* got one   (a) at first; (b) carefully; (c) at last

7. *factory* workers   (a) place where prisoners are kept; (b) building where things are made; (c) army base

8. *hauled* it in   (a) flew; (b) threw; (c) pulled or dragged

---

WORD BUILDING

The word *reported* in the story above means *told*. It can be broken down into three parts:

BEGINNING: *re*

MIDDLE: *port*

END: *ed*

Words are built up around a middle part. Some words may not have any part before or after the middle. For example, the word *say* is a middle part only.

We call the middle part of a word the STEM. Anything added before the stem is called a PREFIX. Anything added after is called a SUFFIX.

21

When looked at separately, these word parts almost always keep the same meaning. Yet when they are put together they make different words. For example, the stem *port* in *reported* always means to carry. *Re* always means either *back* or *again*. Do you remember what *ed* means?

Let's see what REPORTED means when we break down the parts again:

RE means *back*.

PORT means *carry*.

ED means *past tense*.

REPORTED therefore means *carry back in past tense,* or *carried back*.

How does a word which means *carried back* come to mean *told*?

Suppose you had received some news, and brought that news to a friend. You "carried" that news back to him—therefore, you "told" him.

To Do: A number of words are built up around the stem *port* meaning *to carry*. A few of these *port* words are used in column A below. For each of these words, pick out the proper meaning in column B.

A	B
1. *portable* typewriter	(a) send (or carry) away to
2. *import* bananas into	(b) a person who writes the news
3. *export* cars to	
4. *reporter* for a newspaper	(c) a person whose job is to carry things
5. *porter* carries the bags	(d) bring (or carry) into
	(e) able to be carried

EXPRESSING YOURSELF

1. Tell what you would do if you were to see an object that looked like a flying saucer.
2. Suppose you were a reporter sent to speak with someone who has just come from another planet. Prepare three questions to ask that visitor.
3. You have just been invited by a strange-looking man to get on a flying saucer. Tell whether you would get on, and why.
4. Write a paragraph telling why you believe, or do not believe, that there really are flying saucers.

5. THE TURTLE WITH TWO HEADS

"TWO HEADS ARE BETTER THAN ONE," SOME PEOPLE SAY.

READ THIS STORY AND THEN TELL
IF YOU AGREE WITH THAT SAYING.

The Staten Island Zoo in New York City has a two-headed turtle.

The two heads *battle* with one another for food. They also *disagree* on where they want to go.

The turtle *often* tries to walk off in two *direc-*

24

tions at once. It can neither walk nor swim very well.

A turtle born this way has so much *trouble* making up its mind that it does not live very long. Faster-thinking animals looking for food would make short work of a turtle that is unable to agree with itself.

—— NEW YORK TIMES

CHECK YOUR UNDERSTANDING

1. Another title that would best explain the main idea of this story is:
   (a) The Two-Headed Turtle
   (b) Turtles
   (c) The Staten Island Zoo
   (d) Two Heads Are Better Than One
2. The two-headed turtle
   (a) lives long.
   (b) is fast-thinking.
   (c) can be found at the Staten Island Zoo.
   (d) swims well.
3. The two heads of the turtle
   (a) talk to each other.
   (b) fight with each other for food.
   (c) always agree on where they want to go.
   (d) are different in size.
4. The two-headed turtle does not live long because
   (a) turtles do not live long.
   (b) it can't make up its minds fast enough.
   (c) it doesn't swim well.
   (d) it doesn't walk well.

REACHING OUT

From reading this story, we can best say that
(a) there is only one two-headed turtle at the Staten Island Zoo.
(b) two heads are better than one.
(c) two heads are never better than one.
(d) the two-headed turtle is an ugly animal.

FIND THE MISSING WORD

In your notebook, complete the following sentences with words from the story. You may look back at the story.

1. There is a two-headed _____ in the Staten Island Zoo.
2. The two heads of the turtle fight with one another for _____.
3. The turtle cannot walk very _____.
4. The two-headed turtle does not _____ long.
5. This turtle is easily eaten by faster-thinking _____ _____.

IMPROVING YOUR VOCABULARY

In the first column on the next page are the five words in italics from the story. Pick out the best "story" meaning of each of these words.

1. the two heads *battle* (a) shake; (b) fight; (c) eat
2. they *disagree* (a) have different ideas; (b) have the same idea; (c) change their minds
3. *often* walks (a) never; (b) always; (c) many times
4. moves in two *directions* (a) ways to go; (b) legs; (c) streets
5. has *trouble* (a) easiness; (b) difficulty; (c) speed

WORD BUILDING

The word *disagree* in the story above means *not agreeing* or *not having the same opinion.*

The prefix *dis* always means *not,* or *do the opposite of.*

To Do: In your notebook, write the meaning of each of these words that begin with the prefix *dis.* The first one is done for you.

1. dishonest—not honest
2. disrespect
3. disbelieve
4. dislike
5. distrust

A Little Harder: Match the meaning in column B to the proper *dis* word in column A.

A	B
1. *disobey* the rule	(a) stop
2. had a *disease*	(b) not be seen any more

3. *discontinue* a program	(c) not to carry out orders
4. *disappear* from school	(d) illness
5. *disprove* his answer	(e) show something to be false

EXPRESSING YOURSELF

1. Some people act as if they have two heads that disagree. Tell about some person you know who always has trouble making up his mind.
2. Two heads didn't help this turtle. Can you think of some change in the human body that might help us get along better? Tell about the changes you would make if you had the power to make the human body over.
3. Do you know someone who will never change his mind, no matter what you say to him? When would this be a good thing and when would it be bad?
4. Write a paragraph about a time when you had trouble making up your mind.

Continued on Page 18, Column

REVIEW OF LESSONS 1-5

IMPROVING YOUR VOCABULARY

It is time to stop and review the most important words from the first five lessons. Choose the
correct meaning of each of the words below. (The
number in parentheses after each word tells you the
number of the lesson where the word first appeared.)

1. area (4)   (a) building where things
   are made; (b) place where
   soldiers stay; (c) neighborhood

2. attached (3)   (a) found out; (b) brought;
   (c) joined

3. balance (2)   (a) condition of not falling
   over; (b) way to go; (c)
   something that flies

4. base (1)   (a) soft spot of ground; (b) place where soldiers stay; (c) game

5. battle (5)   (a) break; (b) cover; (c) fight

6. captured (4)   (a) took prisoner; (b) lifted; (c) told about

7. customer (3)   (a) scolder; (b) person who buys; (c) person who sells

8. destroyed (1)   (a) found out; (b) tried again; (c) killed

9. directions (5)   (a) talks; (b) ways to go; (c) places to stay

10. disagree (5)   (a) have different ideas; (b) have the same idea; (c) get together

11. discovered (1)   (a) let go; (b) found out for the first time; (c) got

12. factory (4)   (a) building where things are made; (b) quickly-told story; (c) the end of a bus line

13. fills (3)   (a) does not get passing marks; (b) puts in as much as possible; (c) wears away

14. finally (4)   (a) at last; (b) easily; (c) quickly

15. fractured (2)   (a) happened on; (b) carried; (c) broke

16. hauled (4)   (a) yelled to; (b) carried; (c) hit with force

17. items (3)   (a) troubles; (b) objects; (c) places

18. object (4)   (a) thing; (b) bird; (c) plane

19. often (5)   (a) gave; (b) badly; (c) many times

20. patch (2)   (a) object; (b) piece of ground; (c) fracture

21. raised (1)   (a) brought up; (b) hit hard; (c) found out

22. received (3)   (a) joined; (b) let out; (c) got

23. released (3)   (a) let out; (b) found fault with; (c) killed

24. reported (4)   (a) tried again; (b) told; (c) took prisoner

25. scolded (2)   (a) found fault with; (b) broke; (c) went off

26. seriously (2)   (a) carefully; (b) dangerously; (c) softly

27. slammed (3)   (a) hit with force; (b) found fault with; (c) let out

28. strange (4)   (a) mean; (b) pushed back; (c) not seen before

29. surprise (3)   (a) something not expected; (b) difficulty; (c) something found out

30. trouble (5)   (a) way to go; (b) difficulty; (c) a fight

31. vicious (1)   (a) wanting more; (b) mean; (c) not happy

WORD BUILDING

Match the meaning in column B to the proper word-building part in column A.

A	B
1. *ed* (3)	(a) a person who
2. *dis* (5)	(b) shows a happening in
3. *er, or* (1)	the past
4. *un* (2)	(c) do the opposite of
5. *port* (4)	(d) not
	(e) carry

A Little Harder

Match the meaning in column B to the proper word in column A.

A	B
1. disappear (5)	(a) not working
2. unemployed (2)	(b) able to be carried
3. uninjured (2)	(c) person who writes the
4. portable (4)	news
5. disobey (5)	(d) illness
6. unlike (2)	(e) not be seen any more
7. import (4)	(f) stop
8. disease (5)	(g) not listen to
9. discontinue (5)	(h) carry or bring into
10. reporter (4)	(i) different from
	(j) not hurt

6. GIGGLING AUTO MECHANICS

CAN A GIRL BE AS GOOD AN AUTOMOBILE MECHANIC AS A BOY?

THIS STORY MIGHT HELP YOU MAKE UP YOUR MIND.

RUMSON, N.J., May 31 (UPI) — The high school here has a class in taking care of automobiles.

Usually, only boys are in such classes, but this year two girls are learning to *repair* automobiles.

How are they doing? Would you be surprised to find out that their teacher says they learn faster than the boys? They pay closer *attention* and are more careful when they handle the cars.

The teacher *added,* however, that even with grease guns in their hands, girls still *giggle.*

— ST. LOUIS POST-DISPATCH

CHECK YOUR UNDERSTANDING

1. Another title that would best explain the main idea of this story is:
   (a) Girls and Cars
   (b) Girls in an Auto Repair Class
   (c) Giggling Girls
   (d) Girls Who Learn Faster
2. Which of the following is true about the high school in the story?
   (a) Girls are always in the automobile repair class.
   (b) This is the first year the school has a class in automobile repair.
   (c) Girls have been put in an automobile repair class this year for the first time.
   (d) Girls are not allowed in an automobile repair class.
3. The class told about in the story learns
   (a) automobile driving.
   (b) automobile selling.
   (c) automobile repair.
   (d) automobile making.
4. The teacher of the class says that the girls
   (a) do not pay attention.
   (b) learn more slowly than the boys.

(c) are careless in handling cars.

(d) learn faster than the boys.

REACHING OUT

1. The girls told about in the story do *not*
   (a) learn faster.
   (b) teach the class.
   (c) pay closer attention.
   (d) take more care when they handle the cars.
2. The last paragraph of the story shows that:
   (a) though the girls are in a class that is usually for boys only, the girls still act like girls.
   (b) girls cannot do automobile repair work well.
   (c) grease guns make girls giggle.
   (d) the teacher does not like to have girls in his class.

FIND THE MISSING WORD

Fill in the blanks. Complete the following sentences with words from the story, and write the words in your notebook. You may look back at the story.

1. The high school has a _____ in taking care of automobiles.
2. Two girls are _____ to repair automobiles.
3. The girls learn _____ than the boys.
4. The girls are more _____ when they handle cars.
5. The _____ said that the girls giggle.

IMPROVING YOUR VOCABULARY

In the first column below are the five words in italics from the story. Pick out the best "story" meaning of each of these words.

1. *usually* for boys   (a) most of the time; (b) once; (c) always
2. learn to *repair* cars   (a) buy; (b) fix; (c) paint
3. giving *attention* to   (a) money; (b) care and thought; (c) back and forth
4. the teacher *added*   (a) tried; (b) said further; (c) yelled
5. girls *giggle*   (a) talk too much; (b) cry; (c) laugh in a silly way

---

WORD BUILDING

The word *careful* in the above story means *full of care*. A careful person does not rush into anything or take chances.

The letters *ful* at the end of a word almost always mean *full of*.

To Do: In your notebook, write the meaning of each of these words that end in *ful*. The first one is done for you.

    1. beautiful — full of beauty
    2. wonderful
    3. restful
    4. helpful
    5. wasteful

A Little Harder: Match the word in column B to the proper *ful* word in column A.

A	**B**
1. *watchful* for cars	(a) more than enough
2. *grateful* for help	(b) sad
3. *plentiful* rain	(c) careful
4. *mindful* of the last	(d) thankful
time	(e) thinking
5. a *sorrowful* happening	

EXPRESSING YOURSELF

1. Tell why you think an auto repair class for girls would or would not be a good thing.
2. Tell whether you think boys should study cooking and sewing in school.
3. It has been said, "You can't tell a boy from a girl anymore." Write your thoughts on that subject in a paragraph.

7. A MACHINE TO MAKE THE BEDS

WHAT IS A ROBOT?

DO YOU THINK ROBOTS MIGHT SOMEDAY TAKE OVER MOST OF THE WORK THAT MEN AND WOMEN DO?

Would your mother like to have a machine do all her housework?

Don't laugh! There may be such a machine within the next ten years.

A *professor* from England says that the *aver-*

age family will someday be able to buy a *mechanical* housemaid for $2,000.

The machine would look like a box that has mechanical arms and three legs attached to it.

It would be able to set the table, make the beds, push a vacuum cleaner to pick up dust and dirt, and *prepare* vegetables.

The professor said, "I wouldn't want to teach the machine to cook — because wives *enjoy* that."

— REUTERS

CHECK YOUR UNDERSTANDING

1. The main idea of this story is:
   (a) A mechanical housemaid may be in many homes within ten years.
   (b) Machines cannot cook.
   (c) Machines can be bought at as low a price as $2,000.
   (d) Mothers today do not like housework.
2. The machine in this story will look like a
   (a) housemaid.
   (b) automobile.
   (c) vacuum cleaner.
   (d) box.
3. The machine told about in this story
   (a) is already owned by many families.
   (b) will be able to cook.
   (c) will have three legs.
   (d) will not be able to make beds.
4. The professor would not want to teach the machine to cook because
   (a) women like to cook.

(b) it wouldn't work.

(c) the machine would then cost too much.

(d) the food would not taste good.

REACHING OUT

1. The machine told about in this story would *not*

(a) cost about $2,000.

(b) teach other machines.

(c) be in some homes within the next ten years.

(d) have mechanical arms and legs.

2. Which one of the following statements is true?

(a) Everybody agrees that in ten years there will be a mechanical housemaid like the one in this story.

(b) The facts in this story come from an English professor.

(c) A machine like the one told about here will be owned by everybody someday.

(d) Nobody believes that the machine will ever work.

FIND THE MISSING WORD

Fill in the blanks. Complete the following sentences with words from the story and write the words in your notebook. You may look back at the story.

1. The machine would do all of your mother's

_____.

2. Such a machine may be in homes within the next ten _____.

3. The machine would look _____ a box.

4. The machine would be able to set the _____.

5. The machine could _____ a vacuum cleaner.

IMPROVING YOUR VOCABULARY

In the first column below are the five words in italics from the story. Pick out the best "story" meaning of each of these words.

1. a *professor*   (a) housewife; (b) student; (c) college teacher

2. *average* family   (a) rich; (b) older; (c) like most others

3. a *mechanical* housemaid   (a) done or worked by a machine; (b) very good; (c) lazy and careless

4. *prepare* vegetables   (a) make ready; (b) eat; (c) throw away

5. *enjoy* cooking   (a) dislike; (b) be happy with; (c) be unable to do

---

WORD BUILDING

The word *mechanical* in the story above means *having to do with a machine.* If you are good at mechanical things, it means that you are good with things having to do with machines.

41

The letters *al* at the end of a word often mean *having to do with.*

To Do: Write the meaning of each of these words that end in *al*. The first word is done for you.

1. bridal — having to do with a bride
2. musical
3. parental
4. coastal
5. rental

A Little Harder: Sometimes *al* is added to a word part which comes from another language. For example, what do you think *legal* means?

You might have said that *legal* means having to do with a leg! That would have been a good guess, but it is not right. *Leg* in *legal* comes from a Latin word that means *law. Legal,* then, means *having to do with the law.*

Match the meaning in column B to the proper *al* word in column A.

A	**B**
1. *dental* care	(a) having to do with the mind
2. *mental* health	(b) having to do with a king
3. *nasal* bones	(c) having to do with the voice
4. *vocal music*	(d) having to do with the teeth
5. *royal* family	(e) having to do with the nose

EXPRESSING YOURSELF

1. Tell whether you think a machine that could do housework would be good or bad.
2. What three things would you most like to have a machine do for you? Why?

3. If all your work were done by a machine, how would you spend your time?
4. Write a paragraph telling what the world would be like if machines did all the work for men.

8. RAINING FROGS

READ THE FIRST THREE PARAGRAPHS OF THIS STORY. IF YOU WERE MR. LEE, WOULD YOU HAVE THOUGHT IT WAS REALLY RAINING FROGS?

IF NOT, HOW WOULD YOU EXPLAIN FROGS DROPPING LIKE RAIN?

During a very heavy rain, did you ever hear someone say, "It's raining cats and dogs"?

Of course that's just a saying because it isn't *really* raining cats and dogs. Once, Mr. and Mrs. Robert Lee were caught in a bad storm — and they thought it was raining frogs!

They were driving along on a New England road during the storm. They *noticed* that the road was covered with frogs. Mr. Lee stopped the car and a few frogs fell, like raindrops, into his open hands.

(DO NOT READ ON UNTIL YOU HAVE THOUGHT ABOUT AND ANSWERED THE QUESTIONS ON PAGE 44.)

The frogs were not really raining from the sky. They were a type of frog, *common* in New England, that lives in trees. It holds onto the branches of trees with the help of sticky pads on its toes. Sometimes, during heavy storms, the frogs are knocked off the trees and are carried long *distances*. As they fall to the ground, it seems as if it is really raining frogs.

— NEWSDAY (Long Island, N.Y.)

CHECK YOUR UNDERSTANDING

1. Another title that would best explain the main idea of this story is:
   (a) It Was Really Raining Frogs
   (b) Raining Cats and Dogs
   (c) New England Frogs
   (d) Tree Frogs in the Rain
2. The frogs
   (a) were really raining from the sky.
   (b) were catching raindrops.
   (c) were falling from the trees.

(d) were driving along on a New England road.
3. Mr. and Mrs. Lee thought it was raining frogs because
   (a) the road was covered with frogs.
   (b) it wasn't raining cats and dogs.
   (c) they saw them on the trees.
   (d) it was raining very heavily.
4. The Lees saw a kind of frog that holds on to branches of trees
   (a) by its toes.
   (b) only when it rains.
   (c) by its nose.
   (d) for long distances.
5. Which of these sentences is true?
   (a) It sometimes rains cats and dogs.
   (b) It sometimes really rains frogs.
   (c) All frogs live in trees.
   (d) One kind of New England frog lives in trees.

REACHING OUT

You would most likely see the frogs fall off trees
(a) when the sun is shining.
(b) during a rain shower.
(c) when it snows.
(d) during a heavy rain.

FIRST THINGS FIRST

Arrange these events in the order in which they happened.

46

1. Mr. and Mrs. Lee noticed that the road was *2*
   covered with frogs.
2. The Lees were driving along a New England *1*
   road during a very bad storm.
3. Mr. Lee caught a few frogs in his hands. *4*
4. Mr. Lee stopped the car. *3*

IMPROVING YOUR VOCABULARY

In the first column below are the five words in
italics from the story. Pick out the best "story"
meaning of each of these words.

1. *during* the rain (a) at the start; (b) at
   some time in; (c) at the
   end
2. *really* raining (a) hardly; (b) almost;
   (c) truly
3. *noticed* the frogs (a) thought; (b) said; (c)
   saw
4. *common* frog (a) often met with; (b)
   small; (c) hard to find
5. long *distance* (a) in the air; (b) off to
   the side; (c) space between
   two places

WORD BUILDING

The word *it's* in the story above is a short form
of the two words *it is*. When two words are shortened into one by leaving out a letter or two, we call
the shortened word a contraction. To show that one

47

or more letters have been left out, we use the apostrophe (') where the missing letter or letters would be.

Example: In *it's,* the apostrophe is used in place of the missing *i.*

Isn't in the story is a contraction of *is not.* The apostrophe is used in place of the missing *o.*

To Do: In your notebook, write the two words from which the following contractions have been made. The first one is done for you.

1. aren't — are not	**6.** can't
2. don't	**7.** you'll
3. weren't	**8.** I've
4. I'm	**9.** we'll
5. he's	**10.** you've

A Little Harder: Here are two words commonly used together: now write the contraction. The first one is done for you.

1. has not — hasn't	**6.** here is
2. could not	**7.** let us
3. that is	**8.** there is
4. did not	**9.** would not
5. was not	**10.** we are

EXPRESSING YOURSELF

1. What would you do if all the lights in your city or town were to suddenly go out at night and stay out for a number of hours? (This really happened all over the East in 1965.)

2. The Lees *jumped to the conclusion* that it was raining frogs because they did not know about the tree frog. When you jump to a conclusion, you make up your mind without really knowing all the facts.
3. Write a paragraph telling about a time when you *jumped to a conclusion,* and later found that you were wrong.

9. QUICK THINKING

WHAT IS AN EMERGENCY? HAVE YOU EVER HELPED SOMEONE WHO WAS SUDDENLY IN TROUBLE? WHAT DID YOU DO?

HOW DID MARY ANNE SAVE HER SISTER'S LIFE IN THIS EMERGENCY?

ST. PAUL, Sept. 5 — A ten-year-old girl breathed life into the body of her two-year-old sister.

Mary Anne Gilbert *revived* her sister Alice on Thursday while their mother tried to telephone a doctor and the police for help.

Mary Anne later remembered the fast way she saved her sister's life. She had noticed that her sister, who was ill, had begun to *strangle*. She quickly called her mother. After a *useless effort* to help Alice, Mrs. Gilbert handed the baby to Mary Anne and rushed to phone for help. The baby *appeared* to have stopped breathing.

Mary Anne suddenly decided to start breathing into the baby's mouth. Later, Mary Anne explained that she remembered a newspaper story her mother once read to her about a life being saved by mouth-to-mouth breathing.

"So I thought it might work with Alice," she said.

It did.

— ST. PAUL DISPATCH

CHECK YOUR UNDERSTANDING

1. Another title that would best explain the main idea of this story is:
   (a) A Dying Child
   (b) Ten-Year-Old Girl Saves Baby Sister
   (c) The Value of Memory
   (d) No Help
2. Mrs. Gilbert
   (a) tried to telephone for help.
   (b) told Mary Anne to use mouth-to-mouth breathing.
   (c) was not home.
   (d) was able to help the baby when Alice started to strangle.

3. Mary Anne saved Alice's life because
   (a) her mother called the police.
   (b) the doctor told her what to do.
   (c) she remembered her sister's advice.
   (d) she had a good memory.
4. When Alice started breathing again, Mrs. Gilbert most likely
   (a) scolded Alice.
   (b) was very happy.
   (c) was angry because the police didn't come.
   (d) read Mary Anne another story from the newspaper.

REACHING OUT

1. Alice Gilbert was *not*
   (a) ill.
   (b) two years old.
   (c) saved by her sister.
   (d) saved by her mother.
2. One of the things Mary Anne did *not* do was
   (a) help her sister to breathe.
   (b) see her sister's breathing difficulty.
   (c) remember the story her mother read.
   (d) call the doctor.

FIRST THINGS FIRST

Arrange these events in the order in which they happened.

1. Mary Anne breathed into the mouth of her sister.

2. Mrs. Gilbert telephoned the doctor for help. 5
3. Mary Anne saw her sister strangling. 1
4. The baby appeared to have stopped breathing. 3
5. Mary Anne called her mother. 2
6. Alice began to breathe again. 7
7. Mrs. Gilbert tried to help the baby. 4

IMPROVING YOUR VOCABULARY

In the first column below are the five words in italics from the story. Pick out the best "story" meaning of each of these words.

1. *revived* her sister   (a) carried away; (b) brought to life; (c) put to sleep
2. a winning *effort*   (a) pull; (b) try; (c) move
3. began to *strangle*   (a) choke; (b) hold one's breath; (c) blow air
4. *appeared* sad   (a) looked like or seemed; (b) entered into; (c) walked up
5. *useless* worry   (a) small; (b) without success; (c) important

---

WORD BUILDING

The word *revive* in the story above means *to bring back to life*. The prefix *re* means *back* or *again*. The stem *vive* means *to live*. If you put the two parts together, you will have the meaning *to live again*. Since you do not really live *again*, the meaning of the word has come to be *to bring back to life*.

53

Remember that the prefix *re* has two meanings: *back* and *again*.

Example: what does the prefix *re* mean in each of the following sentences? *Back* or *again*?

1. I want to *refile* the letters.
2. I would like to *return* the book that I borrowed.

Refile means to file *again*. "I want to file the letters *again*."

Return means to bring *back*. "I would like to bring *back* the book that I borrowed."

To Do: Read the sentences carefully. Tell whether the prefix *re* in the words in italics means *back* or *again*.

1. *Retry* the dance step with a little more effort.
2. When new machines are invented, workers must be *retrained* to use them.
3. The bank will allow you to *repay* the loan in a year.
4. John *refilled* my glass three times.
5. Denise wants to *reorder* another piece of cake.

A Little Harder: Change each of the following groups of words to one new word that has the same meaning and begins with *re*. The first one is done for you.

1. make again — remake
2. write again
3. trace back
4. place back
5. test again

EXPRESSING YOURSELF

1. Tell what you would do if you were suddenly faced with a fire or some other emergency in your home.
2. Did a story in a newspaper, magazine or book ever help you in an emergency? What good advice have you read about that might help in an emergency at home?
3. Tell whether you think high school students should have training in first aid. Give your reasons.
4. In a paragraph, tell how you, or someone you know, tried to be helpful in an emergency.

10. A MYSTERY

DO YOU BELIEVE IN GHOSTS?

HOW ELSE WOULD YOU EXPLAIN WHAT HAPPENED TO THE DAVIS FAMILY?

LAKEWOOD, N.J., Sept. 2 — There have been strange happenings in the home of Mr. and Mrs. Alan Davis. A *mysterious* scratching, banging and bumping in the walls of their home has become so strong it has knocked down pictures and lamps.

Investigators have torn the walls apart but have been unable to find the cause of the sounds. They are also trying to find out if troublemakers have been at work.

"We first heard the sounds six weeks ago," said Mrs. Davis. For the next two weeks, the sounds happened regularly—every evening from 9:30 to 11:00.

"Little *patches,*" she said, "began to appear on the living room and bedroom walls." Then the sounds changed and became *irregular.* "Now," she said, "the noises start at 8 A.M. and *continue* on and off till midnight."

— NEW YORK TIMES

CHECK YOUR UNDERSTANDING

1. Another title that would best explain the main idea of this story is:
   (a) Banging and Bumping
   (b) Regular Sounds
   (c) Strange Happenings in a Jersey Home
   (d) Troublemakers
2. The cause of the mysterious scratchings and banging is
   (a) troublemakers.
   (b) not known.
   (c) Mrs. Davis.
   (d) little patches.
3. The sounds
   (a) were first heard two weeks ago.
   (b) always happened in a regular way.
   (c) now start at 9:30 P.M.
   (d) do not happen in a regular way.
4. The events told about in this story
   (a) happened before September 2.
   (b) happened after September 2.
   (c) happened before and after September 2.
   (d) never happened.

REACHING OUT

The scratchings and banging did *not*
(a) cause pictures and lamps to be moved.
(b) mark the walls.
(c) cause trouble for the Davises.
(d) end at the time this story was written.

WHO DID WHAT?

Pick out the words in column B that properly finish the sentences started in column A. The correct answer for the first one is: (c) "Mrs. Davis . . . . first heard the sounds six weeks ago."

A	B
1. Mrs. Davis	(a) may have been at work.
2. Investigators	
3. Troublemakers	(b) were seen on the wall.
4. Little patches	(c) first heard the sounds six weeks ago.
5. Banging and bumping	(d) knocked down pictures.
	(e) tore the walls apart.

IMPROVING YOUR VOCABULARY

In the first column on the next page are the five words in italics from the story. Pick out the best "story" meaning of each of these words.

1. a *mysterious* scratching   (a) dangerous; (b) loud; (c) strange
2. a special *investigator*   (a) a person who collects tickets; (b) a person who looks into a problem carefully; (c) a person who makes trouble
3. little *patches*   (a) rain; (b) spots; (c) dogs
4. *irregular* noises   (a) uneven; (b) loud; (c) smooth
5. *continue* tomorrow   (a) keep on; (b) keep out; (c) keep off

---

WORD BUILDING

The word *continue* in the story means *to keep on*. How did it come to have that meaning? We can learn it by breaking the word down into parts. The prefix *con* means *together* or *with*. The stem *tin* means *to hold. Continue,* therefore, means *to hold together.* When we continue a job, it means that we *hold together* or *keep on* until it is done.

When you see *con* at the beginning of a word, it means *together* or *with.*

To Do: Each of the italicized words in column A on the next page is built up around the prefix *con.* Here is a list of stems and their meanings.

duct	means lead
struct	means build
tain	means hold
vene	means come
tend	means fight

59

Use this list to help you match the meanings in column B to the italicized words in column A.

A	B
1. to *conduct* a band	(a) to build together
2. to *convene* on Saturday	(b) to fight with
3. to *construct* a new house	(c) to lead together
4. to *contend* for the game	(d) to come together
5. to *contain* a surprise in a box	(e) to hold with

A Little Harder: Fill in the blanks. In the sentences below, the words in italics are the meanings of the prefixes and stems used in this lesson. Complete each sentence by choosing the proper "con" word from the following list. Write the word in your notebook.

> conducts
> constructs
> contains
> contend
> convenes

1. When a designer *builds* a model *with* clay, he _____ a model.

2. When boxers *fight with* each other for the championship, they _____ for the championship.

3. When Duke Ellington *leads* the men of his band to play *together,* he _____ them.

4. When the United States Congress *comes together* to talk about the nation's problems, it _____.

5. When the trunk of my car *holds* a spare tire, it _____ the tire.

60

EXPRESSING YOURSELF

1. Thomas Edison, the famous inventor, believed that he would be able to talk with the living after his death. What do you think? Are there such things as ghosts or spirits?
2. The Davis family was no doubt puzzled by these mysterious happenings. Tell about something that has bothered you very much, or "driven you mad."
3. Write a paragraph about some mysterious experience you have had. If you like, you may tell of someone you read or heard about.
4. If you were an investigator called in by Mr. and Mrs. Davis, what steps would you have taken to solve the mystery?

REVIEW OF LESSONS 6-10

IMPROVING YOUR VOCABULARY

Choose the correct meaning of each of the words below. The number in parentheses after each word tells you the number of the lesson where the word first appeared.

1. added (6)
(a) saw; (b) made ready; (c) said further

2. appeared (9)
(a) looked like or seemed; (b) fixed; (c) was happy with

3. attention (6)
(a) try; (b) coming and going; (c) care and thought

4. average (7)
(a) like most others; (b) old; (c) strange

62

5. common (8)   (a) not important; (b) often met with; (c) funny

6. continue (10)   (a) hold off; (b) make ready; (c) keep on or last

7. distance (8)   (a) care and thought; (b) space between two places; (c) spots

8. during (8)   (a) at some time in; (b) uneven; (c) hard

9. effort (9)   (a) worry; (b) space between two places; (c) try

10. enjoy (7)   (a) said further; (b) be happy with; (c) laugh in a silly way

11. giggle (6)   (a) choke; (b) try; (c) laugh in a silly way

12. investigator (10)   (a) person who teaches in a college; (b) person who looks into a problem carefully; (c) person who is learning to repair cars

13. irregular (10)   (a) uneven; (b) not rich; (c) common

14. mechanical (7)   (a) strange; (b) without success; (c) done or worked by a machine

15. mysterious (10)   (a) strange; (b) uneven; (c) like most others

16. noticed (8)   (a) saw; (b) kept on; (c) made ready

17. patches (10)   (a) spots; (b) space between two places; (c) main parts

18. prepare (7)   (a) look like; (b) bring to life; (c) make ready

19. professor (7)   (a) actor; (b) person who looks into a problem carefully; (c) college teacher

20. really (8)   (a) most of the time; (b) truly; (c) often met with

21. repair (6)   (a) fix; (b) see; (c) be happy with

22. revived (9)   (a) looked like; (b) brought to life; (c) got ready

23. strangle (9)   (a) not common; (b) laugh in a silly way; (c) choke

24. useless (9)   (a) uneven; (b) without success; (c) sad

25. usually (6)   (a) truly; (b) most of the time; (c) strangely

---

WORD BUILDING

Match the meaning in column B to the proper word-building part in column A.

A	**B**
1. *al* (7)	(a) full of
2. *con* (10)	(b) having to do with
3. *re* (9)	(c) together, with
4. *ful* (6)	(d) back, again

A Little Harder: Match the meaning in column B to the proper word in column A on the next page. The number in parentheses tells you in which lesson you first saw the word.

	A		**B**
1.	construct (10)	(a)	thankful
2.	sorrowful (6)	(b)	sad
3.	mental (7)	(c)	having to do with the mind
4.	contain (10)		
5.	grateful (6)	(d)	lead together
6.	vocal (7)	(e)	careful
7.	plentiful (6)	(f)	build
8.	conduct (10)	(g)	having to do with the voice
9.	watchful (6)		
10.	dental (7)	(h)	more than enough
		(i)	having to do with the teeth
		(j)	hold

11. A HOUSEWIFE'S "EASY DAY"

WHO WORKS HARDER—THE MAN WHO GOES TO WORK OR HIS WIFE WHO STAYS HOME WITH THE CHILDREN? WHAT WOULD YOUR PARENTS SAY ABOUT THIS SUBJECT?

IS MRS. O'NEILL'S WORK HARD OR EASY?

VANCOUVER, B.C., May 5 — How far does the average housewife travel as she cleans, dusts, washes and chases after the children?

Mrs. Peggy O'Neill took part in an *experiment* to look for an answer. She wore a pedometer for a whole day. A pedometer is something that *measures* how far a person walks. Mrs. O'Neill kept her usual *schedule* during the test.

Her day started at 7:30 A.M. when she made breakfast for her husband and children. She did the dishes, made the beds and drove the children to nursery school.

During the morning she cleaned the bedrooms and bathroom and washed three loads of laundry in the basement. She also went next door to water her neighbor's plants.

She picked up the children at noon, and then

made lunch, *vacuumed* the floors and cleaned the windows. Then came the evening meal for the family, more dishes and a final trip to the basement.

Mrs. O'Neill's *total* walking distance was 7½ miles.

— CANADIAN PRESS

CHECK YOUR UNDERSTANDING

1. Another title that would best explain the main idea of this story is:
   (a) The Work Day of a Housewife
   (b) Housewife Passes Test
   (c) Housewife Runs 7½ Miles
   (d) How to Keep a Clean House
2. Mrs. O'Neill wore a pedometer
   (a) because she looked good in one.
   (b) to find out how far she would walk.
   (c) to help her clean the house.
   (d) because she could work faster with it.
3. Mrs. O'Neill vacuumed the floors
   (a) in the morning.
   (b) after lunch.
   (c) on Tuesday.
   (d) in the evening.
4. Mrs. O'Neill watered her neighbor's plants
   (a) in the evening.
   (b) during the morning.
   (c) after supper.
   (d) when the children came home from school.
5. Mrs. O'Neill starts her day at
   (a) 8:30 P.M.
   (b) 7:30 A.M.

68

(c) 8:00 A.M.
(d) 7:30 P.M.

REACHING OUT

1. In the morning, Mrs. O'Neill did *not* do one of the following:
   (a) drive the children to nursery school.
   (b) make the beds.
   (c) clean the windows.
   (d) wash three loads of laundry.
2. From reading this story, we can best say that:
   (a) Women always walk 7½ miles a day when they do housework.
   (b) A housewife works harder than her husband.
   (c) A housewife may do much walking during her day.
   (d) A husband works harder than his wife.

FIRST THINGS FIRST

Arrange these things in the order in which Mrs. O'Neill did them.

1. She washed three loads of laundry in the basement. 4
2. She made lunch. 7
3. She vacuumed the floors. 5
4. She drove the children to nursery school. 3
5. She got up early in the morning. 1

69

6. She made breakfast at 7:30 A.M. 2

7. She picked up the children at lunch time. 6

IMPROVING YOUR VOCABULARY

In the first column below are the five words in italics from the story. Pick out the best "story" meaning of each of these words.

1. *measures* how far a person walks   (a) finds how much; (b) throws away; (c) walks back

2. her usual *schedule*   (a) way to walk; (b) plan; (c) day off

3. the *total* distance   (a) part of; (b) least; (c) whole

4. *vacuumed* the floors   (a) waxed; (b) wet; (c) cleaned with a special machine

5. an *experiment*   (a) test to find something out; (b) kind of puzzle; (c) long day

---

WORD BUILDING

The word *pedometer* in the story means *something used to measure how far someone walks.* The ending of the word, *meter,* gives you a clue to the meaning of the word. This ending means *to measure.*

You have often seen *meter* used by itself. For example, your "gas meter man" is the man who visits your house to copy from your gas meter the amount of gas your family has used. The gas company can then figure out your bill.

Something that measures, therefore, is a *meter*. When you see this ending on a word, you will know that the word means *something that measures.*

To Do: Can you tell what each of the things in column A measures? Choose the correct meaning for each *meter* word from column B.

A	B
1. a *thermometer*	(a) something that measures how long someone can park his car
2. a *speedometer*	
3. an *electric meter*	
4. a *meter maid*	(b) something that measures how fast a car is going
5. a *parking meter*	
	(c) something that measures how cold or hot a person or thing is
	(d) something that measures how much electricity has been used
	(e) woman who takes care of parking meters

A Little Harder: Match these "meter" words. If you cannot figure out their meaning, use your dictionary.

A	B
1. a *voltmeter*	(a) something that measures how far away a thing is
2. a *barometer*	
3. a *telemeter*	(b) something that meas-

71

ures the power of elec-
tricity
(c) something that meas-
ures the pressure of
the air to help the
weatherman tell about
changes in the weather

EXPRESSING YOURSELF

1. Can a man keep house as well as a woman can?
   Why, or why not?
2. Many jobs or duties that were once done by
   men are now done by women. Give some examples.
3. Men are helping with family or household work
   more than ever before. Give some examples of
   jobs in the home now done by men.
4. Some women say they would rather work hard
   in regular jobs than stay home. Why is this so?

12. THE MAN WHO WOULDN'T SLEEP

HOW LONG DO YOU THINK YOU COULD GO WITHOUT SLEEPING? WHAT DO YOU SUPPOSE IS THE LONGEST TIME ANY MAN HAS STAYED AWAKE?

WOULD YOU LIKE TO TRY TO STAY AWAKE FOR AS LONG AS PETER TRIPP DID?

Jan. 30 — Peter Tripp slept for thirteen hours and thirteen minutes yesterday. He wasn't lazy. He had just gone without sleep for 201 hours and ten minutes.

He still looked tired when he awoke. Doctors who *examined* him said that he was still unable to think *clearly*.

Mr. Tripp said that after being awake for *several* days he began seeing things. He *imagined* that he saw cobwebs, odd shapes and even mice and kittens. Then he knew he had stayed awake too long.

Mr. Tripp is a radio announcer who stayed awake as a test. He was helping *scientists* find out what happens to people who go without sleep for a long time.

He told *reporters* that he would not like to *repeat* his *stunt*.

— NEW YORK TIMES

CHECK YOUR UNDERSTANDING

1. Another title that would best explain the main idea of this story is:
   (a) Seeing Things
   (b) A Stunt
   (c) The Life of a Radio Announcer
   (d) Staying Awake for Science
2. Peter Tripp stayed awake for
   (a) thirteen hours and thirteen minutes.
   (b) more than 200 hours.
   (c) more than 200 days.
   (d) less than 200 hours.
3. Mr. Tripp said that he stayed awake
   (a) to get attention for himself.
   (b) to sell sleeping pills.
   (c) to imagine things.

(d) to help science.

4. Mr. Tripp
   (a) would not like to repeat this test.
   (b) is a reporter.
   (c) said he would like to go without sleep for more than 201 hours and ten minutes.
   (d) is a scientist.

REACHING OUT

1. One of the things Peter Tripp did *not* imagine he saw was
   (a) cobwebs.
   (b) kittens.
   (c) dollar bills.
   (d) mice.

2. After Mr. Tripp awoke, he
   (a) imagined he saw cobwebs.
   (b) thought clearly.
   (c) was not tired.
   (d) was examined by doctors.

FIRST THINGS FIRST

Arrange these things in the order in which Peter Tripp did them.

1. He was examined by doctors.
2. He became a radio announcer.
3. He slept for over thirteen hours.
4. He began a test to see how long he could go without sleep.
5. He imagined that he saw strange things.

IMPROVING YOUR VOCABULARY

In the first column below are the eight words in italics from the story. Pick out the best "story" meaning of each of these words.

1. doctors *examined* him — (a) spoke to; (b) looked at closely; (c) heard
2. think *clearly* — (a) with understanding; (b) incorrectly; (c) without reason
3. *several* days — (a) one; (b) none; (c) more than one
4. he *imagined* — (a) tried to see; (b) complained; (c) saw in his mind
5. *scientists* find out — (a) people who own a business; (b) people who dream a lot; (c) people who try to learn the truth about our world
6. told *reporters* — (a) close friends; (b) people who get news for a newspaper; (c) many times
7. would not *repeat* — (a) talk about; (b) do again; (c) try
8. did a *stunt* — (a) act that makes people watch you; (b) game that people watch; (c) song that people sing

WORD BUILDING

The word *scientist* in the story above means *a person who works in science*. When you see *ist* at

76

the end of a word of more than one syllable, it often means *a person who works in or with*.

Example: *florist* means *a person who works with flowers*.

But: list is a word of one syllable. Here, the *ist* is part of the stem, not an ending. It therefore does *not* mean *a person who works in or with*, as it does in larger words, such as *scientist* and *florist*.

To Do: All of the following words end in *ist*. Copy the words in which the *ist* means *a person who works in or with*.

1. pianist
2. machinist
3. fist
4. dentist
5. wrist

6. twist
7. artist
8. violinist
9. mist
10. druggist

A Little Harder: Next to each of the words you copied write its meaning. The first one is done for you.

1. pianist — a person who works with a piano

EXPRESSING YOURSELF

1. Tell how you felt at some time when you were sleepy but had to stay awake.
2. Tell about someone you know who does "crazy" stunts to get everyone to pay attention to him.
3. Find out how one of these four people helped science by risking his or her life or career: Louis Pasteur; Marie Curie; Galileo; Thor Heyerdahl (HY-ER-DAL). Write a paragraph telling what you found out about that person.
4. Why do scientists sometimes ask people in prison to help them in their experiments?

13. THE ARTIST WAS A TRUANT

MANY STUDENTS WHO STAY AWAY FROM SCHOOL TOO OFTEN FINALLY DROP OUT COMPLETELY.

WHY DO STUDENTS BECOME TRUANTS? CAN A SCHOOL DO ANYTHING TO HELP KEEP THEM FROM BEING TRUANT?

Charles White is one of the top *artists* in America. He is now *probably* the country's best-known Negro artist, who does most of his work about Negro life.

White grew up in Chicago. For his seventh birthday his mother bought him a set of oil paints. One day he pulled down the window shades and used them to paint on. His first prize for painting was a good *spanking* from his mother.

In high school he was often *truant,* until he won a school prize for his art work. Then he began to study art seriously.

While he paints, he listens to music, often the gospel kind that is based on the Bible. "I have to have sounds," he *insists.* "I can't paint in *silence.*"

He never takes a *vacation* from art, for he is unhappy when he is not working.

If a painting doesn't seem right, he will start over again *completely,* "no matter how long I've gone on it or how big it is."

Today a White drawing sells for $1,500. His paintings sell for $1,800 to $2,500.

— EBONY

CHECK YOUR UNDERSTANDING

1. Another title that would best explain the main idea of this story is:
   (a) Painting and Music
   (b) A Truant
   (c) His Prize Was a Spanking
   (d) Charles White: Well-Known Negro Artist
2. Most of Charles White's work is about
   (a) high school.
   (b) Negro life.

(c) childhood.

(d) gospel music.

3. White's mother spanked him because

(a) he used his set of oil paints.

(b) he won a prize.

(c) it was his birthday.

(d) he had painted on the window shades.

4. When White paints

(a) he often listens to music.

(b) he must have music.

(c) he is unhappy.

(d) he sings to himself.

5. White was a truant

(a) all through high school.

(b) after he won a prize for his art work.

(c) before he won a prize for his art work.

(d) because he liked to paint.

REACHING OUT

1. Charles White does *not*

(a) get about $1,500 for a drawing.

(b) listen to music when he paints.

(c) sketch and paint Negro life.

(d) take vacations from art.

2. The next to the last paragraph of the story shows that White

(a) paints only for money.

(b) paints very fast.

(c) wants his work to be perfect.

(d) doesn't really like painting.

FIRST THINGS FIRST

Arrange these things in the order in which they happened to Charles White.

1. He became a top artist.
2. He won a prize in high school for his art.
3. He was truant in high school.
4. He received a spanking from his mother.
<u>**5.**</u> His mother bought him a set of oil paints.

IMPROVING YOUR VOCABULARY

In the first column below and on the next page are the eight words in italics from the story. Pick out the best "story" meaning of each of these words.

1. a top *artist* — (a) successful person; (b) person who draws and paints pictures; (c) person who makes a lot of money

2. *probably* best-known — (a) more likely than not; (b) surely; (c) hardly

3. a good *spanking* — (a) scolding; (b) bath; (c) striking with the open hand

4. often *truant* — (a) doing well in school; (b) staying away from school without permission; (c) winning many prizes

5. he *insists* — (a) asks a question; (b)

81

speaks in a low voice; (c)
takes a strong stand

6. *silence* while
painting

(a) noise; (b) no sound;
(c) darkness

7. takes a *vacation*

(a) time of being free from
school or work; (b) large
sum of money; (c) long
period of time

8. start over
completely

(a) wholly; (b) little by
little; (c) partly

WORD BUILDING

The word *insists* in the story above means
takes a strong stand. If you *insist* on something, it
would be very hard for someone to make you
change your mind.

Explanation: IN means *in* or *into*.
SIST means *stand*.

The word *insist* then means *to stand in*; when
you insist, it would not be easy to move you from
where you "stand."

The prefix *in* at the start of a word often means
in or *into*.

Example: The word *inspect* means to look
into.

To Do: Match the meaning in column B to
the proper *in* word in column A.

A	**B**
1. a year's *income*	(a) put air into
2. go *indoors*	(b) breathe in
3. the *inmost* part	(c) money coming in

4. *inflate* the tire   (d) in a house or building

5. *inhale* smoke   (e) farthest in

A Little Harder: Sometimes *in* at the start of a word means *not*. For example, *invisible* means *not able to be seen.*

For each of the following *in* words, write *into* in your notebook if the meaning is *in* or *into*. Write *not* if the meaning is *not.*

    1. invite
    2. incomplete
    3. incorrect
    4. inhuman
    5. inside

EXPRESSING YOURSELF

1. In this story Charles White remembers something that happened when he was seven years old. In a paragraph, tell some childhood memory that stands out in your mind.

2. What stopped White from being a truant? What ideas do you have for keeping students from "playing hookey"?

3. White likes gospel music. What is your favorite kind of music, and why?

4. "If his work doesn't feel right, he will start over again completely." White wants his work to be just right — perfect — even if it causes him all kinds of trouble. Are you like that? Is it a good way to be? Why, or why not?

5. Charles White likes his work so much he never takes a vacation from it. Tell of a job you'd like to have that you'd really enjoy.

14. LOST IN A CAVE

WERE YOU EVER IN A DANGEROUS SPOT ALL BY YOURSELF? HOW DID YOU FEEL?

DID BILL DEAN "USE HIS HEAD" WHEN HE WAS IN DANGER?

GOSPORT, Ind., Sept. 28 (UPI) — A 17-year-old cave *explorer* was *rescued,* wet and cold, today. He had been *trapped* for twenty-three hours without food or light inside a *narrow* part of a cave.

Bill Dean had gone exploring by himself yesterday afternoon with only a lamp to light his way. Less than an hour after he *entered* the cave, his light went out.

He sat in the *damp* darkness the rest of the day, all night and part of today. "I was a little bit scared," Bill said.

He had *decided* against trying to find his way out. He thought it best to wait for somebody to rescue him.

One boy *crawled* 600 feet into the cave, but could not find Bill.

Finally, one of Bill's friends and a teacher crawled slowly inside, found him and led him to safety.

— INDIANAPOLIS STAR

CHECK YOUR UNDERSTANDING

1. Another title that would best explain the main idea of this story is:
   (a) Exploring Caves
   (b) An Unwise Boy
   (c) Twenty-Three Hours of Danger
   (d) Fear!
2. Bill Dean was trapped in the cave because
   (a) he went in alone.
   (b) his light went out.
   (c) he became afraid.
   (d) he had no food.
3. Bill was rescued by
   (a) a friend and a teacher.
   (b) the first person who tried to save him.
   (c) a team of twenty-three men.
   (d) crawling out of the cave himself.
4. Before he was rescued, Bill
   (a) had food left.
   (b) was warm and dry.
   (c) had a working flashlight.
   (d) was alone.
5. After the rescue, Bill most likely
   (a) went back into the cave.
   (b) had something to eat.
   (c) went dancing.
   (d) got angry with the boy who had not rescued him.

REACHING OUT

1. Bill was rescued in the
   (a) morning.
   (b) afternoon.
   (c) evening.
   (d) night.
2. Bill thought it best not to crawl out himself because
   (a) he was too scared.
   (b) he would probably never get out without a light.
   (c) his friends yelled to him to stay where he was.
   (d) he was too hungry.

FIRST THINGS FIRST

Arrange these things in the order in which they happened to Bill.
1. His light went out.
2. One boy crawled into the cave, but could not find him.
3. He was rescued.
4. He sat in the damp darkness of the cave.
5. He went exploring the cave by himself.

IMPROVING YOUR VOCABULARY

In the first column below are the eight words in italics from the story. Pick out the best "story" meaning of each of these words.

1. a cave *explorer*   (a) person who gets lost easily; (b) person who has bad luck; (c) person who goes to little known places

2. was *rescued*   (a) saved; (b) lost; (c) sent away

3. *trapped* in a cave   (a) lost; (b) found after a long time; (c) caught without a way of getting out

4. *narrow* part   (a) wide; (b) not wide; (c) deep

5. *entered* the cave   (a) went out of; (b) went into; (c) fell into

6. *damp* darkness   (a) a little wet; (b) very cold; (c) bringing fear

7. *decided* to wait   (a) asked; (b) fought; (c) made up his mind

8. *crawled* in   (a) walked straight; (b) ran quickly; (c) moved slowly on hands and knees

WORD BUILDING

The word *darkness* in the story above means *a state of being dark*. The word-ending *ness* always means *a state of being*.

88

Example: *Lateness* means *a state of being late*.

To Do: Write the meaning of each of these words ending in *ness* in your notebook. The first one is done for you.
1. kindness — a state of being kind
2. quickness
3. redness
4. sickness
5. sweetness

A Little Harder: Many words ending in *y* change the *y* to *i* before *ness*. Write the meaning of each of these words. The first word is done for you.
1. happiness — a state of being happy
2. earliness
3. easiness
4. prettiness
5. readiness

A Little Harder: These are five words ending in *ness*.

tallness   coolness   stillness   whiteness   smallness

Use one of these words to complete each sentence below.

1. The _____ of the room made it hard to move about.
2. The _____ of the night was broken by a cry.
3. There is nothing quite like the _____ of snow.
4. His _____ helped him to reach the top shelf.
5. The _____ of the day made me wish I had my coat.

89

EXPRESSING YOURSELF

1. Tell about someone you know or read about who kept calm in a dangerous spot. What did he do? What would have happened if he had "lost his head"?
2. Is it possible to know beforehand whether a certain person would be brave in a dangerous spot? How?
3. What natural or historic places in or around your city would you like to visit? See your city directory, museum or library to find out what places exist.
4. Tell in a paragraph of a dangerous spot you once found yourself in.

15. men on THE moon

WHEN YOU SAW PICTURES OF THE MOON DID YOU WISH YOU COULD BE THERE?

WHAT CAN YOU FIND OUT FROM THIS STORY ABOUT LIVING ON THE MOON?

For thousands of years men have dreamed about going to the moon. Now men have landed on it but living there will not be easy.

The moon is a dead world, without air and water. It is hit by *dangerous* rays.

Man has lived on the earth under very hard *conditions*. At the South Pole men have lived for many months in *temperatures* of 75 to 100 *degrees* below zero!

Living on the moon will be even harder than living at the South Pole. Each night is two weeks long and the temperature drops to 200 degrees below zero. Each day is two weeks long, but the temperature rises to 200 degrees above zero.

If man hopes to live on the moon, he will have to make his houses there strong and *airtight*. Instead of building up, he will have to build down. He will have to dig beneath the moon's *surface* and live underground.

91

The first men on the moon had to carry along their own air, water and food with them from the earth. Later, when men live on the moon, *spaceships* will have to keep bringing in more *supplies*.

After a while, man might be able to find ways to get his air, food and water supplies from the moon itself.

— "Ask Uncle Ray," ST. LOUIS POST-DISPATCH

CHECK YOUR UNDERSTANDING

1. Another title that would best explain the main idea of this story is:
   (a) Life at the South Pole
   (b) Long Days and Nights
   (c) Hard Life on the Moon
   (d) Moon Beams
2. Living on the moon will be
   (a) easy.
   (b) just like living at the South Pole.
   (c) safe.
   (d) hard.
3. The moon
   (a) is hit by dangerous rays.
   (b) has air.
   (c) has water.
   (d) has its own food supply.
4. A night on the moon will
   (a) last for two weeks.
   (b) be 200 degrees above zero.
   (c) be less cold than at the South Pole.
   (d) be the same temperature as during the day.

5. Temperatures on the moon are
  (a) the same as those on the earth.
  (b) the same as at the South Pole.
  (c) hot in the day and hot at night.
  (d) hot in the day and cold at night.

REACHING OUT

1. Houses on the moon will *not* be
  (a) airtight.
  (b) strong.
  (c) underground.
  (d) many stories high.
2. The first men on the moon had to bring their own air, water and food because
  (a) they are used to that of the earth.
  (b) there is none on the moon.
  (c) spaceships will bring in more later.
  (d) they will be able to get their own supply later.

PUTTING THE PIECES TOGETHER

Below and on the next page are titles for each of the seven paragraphs in the story. Put these titles in the order that the paragraphs appear in the story. The first two are done for you.

1. Days and Nights on the Moon
2. Four Facts about the Moon — Paragraph 2

3. Houses on the Moon
4. A Dream of Going to the Moon — Paragraph 1
5. Air, Water and Food from Earth
6. Air, Water and Food from the Moon
7. Temperatures at the South Pole

IMPROVING YOUR VOCABULARY

In the first column below and on the next page are the eight words in italics from the story. Pick out the best "story" meaning of each of these words.

1. *dangerous* rays   (a) wild; (b) bright; (c) unsafe

2. hard *conditions*   (a) the way things are; (b) the kinds of people; (c) the kinds of weather

3. low *temperature*   (a) kind of place; (b) amount of heat; (c) houses

4. 75 *degrees*   (a) laws of a country; (b) number of times; (c) units for measuring amount of heat

5. *airtight* houses   (a) not letting air in or out; (b) open air; (c) empty

6. *surface* of the moon   (a) inside; (b) center; (c) outside

7. *spaceship* to the moon   (a) ship or plane going to outer space; (b) boat with plenty of room; (c) people going to outer space

95

8. bring in *supplies*   (a) people to help; (b) things needed; (c) air for breathing

---

WORD BUILDING

The word *dangerous* in the story means *full of danger*. The letters *ous* at the end of a word almost always mean *full of*.

To Do: Write the meaning of each of these words ending in *ous* in your notebook. The first one is done for you.

1. glamorous — full of glamor
2. joyous
3. poisonous
4. thunderous
5. mountainous

A Little Harder: Match the meaning in column B to the proper *ous* word in column A.

A	B
1. *famous* man	(a) brave
2. *humorous* story	(b) sweet-sounding
3. *melodious* song	(c) very well-known
4. *spacious* room	(d) funny
5. *courageous* soldier	(e) large

EXPRESSING YOURSELF

1. Tell whether or not you would like to go to the moon. If your library has them, find pictures of

the moon. Then write a paragraph describing its surface.

2. Tell about the house you would want to build for yourself on the moon. (You may draw it, or even build a model of it.)

3. If you were the President of our country, would you spend billions of dollars to put men on Mars? If not, what other uses for the money could you give?

4. Imagine that you have just arrived on the moon. Write a letter back home to a relative or friend telling about your first day on the moon.

REVIEW OF LESSONS 11-15

IMPROVING YOUR VOCABULARY

Choose the correct meaning of each of the words below. (The number in parentheses after each word is the number of the lesson where the word first appeared.)

1. airtight (15)   (a) a little wet; (b) not letting air in or out; (c) closely watched

2. artist (13)   (a) person who draws or paints pictures; (b) test to find something out; (c) person who gets news for a newspaper

3. clearly (12)   (a) with understanding; (b) at last; (c) completely

4. completely (13)   (a) narrowly; (b) wetly; (c) totally

5. condition (15) (a) act that makes people watch you; (b) the way things are; (c) unit for measuring the amount of heat

6. crawled (14) (a) moved slowly on hands and knees; (b) made up one's mind; (c) caught without a way of getting out

7. damp (14) (a) not wide; (b) a little wet; (c) safe

8. dangerous (15) (a) not wide; (b) more likely than not; (c) not safe

9. decided (14) (a) took a vacation; (b) looked at closely; (c) made up one's mind

10. degrees (15) (a) units for measuring amount of heat; (b) people who get news for a newspaper; (c) children who stay away from school without permission

11. entered (14) (a) saw in the mind; (b) took a strong stand; (c) went into

12. examined (12) (a) looked at closely; (b) saved; (c) made to keep quiet

13. experiment (11) (a) plan; (b) something needed; (c) test to find something out

14. explorer (14) (a) person who tries to learn the truth about our world; (b) person who goes to little-known places; (c)

99

person who gets news for a
newspaper

15. imagined (12) (a) saw in the mind; (b)
moved slowly on hands and
knees; (c) planned

16. insists (13) (a) takes a strong stand;
(b) does again; (c) finds
out how much

17. measures (11) (a) goes into; (b) saves;
(c) finds out how much

18. narrow (14) (a) not wide; (b) not safe;
(c) whole

19. probably (13) (a) with understanding;
(b) more likely than not;
(c) safely

20. repeat (12) (a) save; (b) do again; (c)
strike with an open hand

21. reporters (12) (a) airplanes going to outer
space; (b) people who go
to little known places; (c)
people who get news for a
newspaper

22. rescued (14) (a) saved; (b) let in; (c)
did again

23. schedule (11) (a) outside; (b) something
needed; (c) plan

24. scientists (12) (a) people who do dangerous things; (b) people who
try to learn the truth about
our world; (c) people who
draw and paint pictures

25. several (12) (a) not wide; (b) more
than one; (c) outside

26. silence (13) (a) no sound; (b) amount
of heat; (c) plan

27. spaceships (15)   (a) strange boats; (b) great dangers; (c) ships going to outer space

28. spanking (13)   (a) acting to make people watch you; (b) striking with the open hand; (c) moving slowly on hands and knees

29. stunt (12)   (a) an act that makes people watch you; (b) test to find something out; (c) plan

30. supplies (15)   (a) units for measuring amount of heat; (b) something not looked for; (c) things needed

31. surface (15)   (a) the way things are; (b) outside; (c) child who stays away from school without permission

32. temperature (15)   (a) anger; (b) amount of heat; (c) no sound

33. total (11)   (a) part of; (b) least; (c) whole

34. trapped (14)   (a) saved; (b) airtight; (c) caught without a way of getting out

35. truant (13)   (a) staying away from school without permission; (b) trying to find out the truth; (c) finding something out

36. vacation (13)   (a) plan for future action; (b) time of being free from school or work; (c) an act

that makes people watch you

37. vacuum (11)   (a) clean with a special machine; (b) strike with the open hand; (c) look at very closely

---

WORD BUILDING

Match the meaning in column B to the correct word-building part in column A.

A	**B**
1. *ness* (14)	(a) measure
2. *ist* (12)	(b) full of
3. *in* (13)	(c) person who works with
4. *ous* (15)	(d) state of being
5. *meter* (11)	(e) into, or not

A Little Harder: Match the meaning in column B to the proper word in column A.

A	**B**
1. income	(a) funny
2. famous	(b) sweet-sounding
3. melodious	(c) breathe in
4. barometer	(d) measure of heat
5. humorous	(e) very well-known
6. inflate	(f) money coming in
7. courageous	(g) large
8. thermometer	(h) measure of air pressure
9. spacious	(i) put air into
10. inhale	(j) brave

102

WRAPPING IT UP: A REVIEW OF LESSONS 1-15

a child sho... not obey his parents?

Priscilla Brown is a very good child. She is only six years old but is responsible and obedient. She takes excellent care of her four younger brothers and never disobeys her mother. Since yesterday, however, Mrs. Mary Brown, her mother, probably thinks she is a little too obedient.

The Browns live in the third floor of an apartment house in Brooklyn. Roderick Thompson, four years old, lives in an adjoining apartment. At 9 A.M. yesterday, Roderick noticed smoke curling from under the Browns' door. He called his mother, Mrs. Sophie Thompson, who rang the doorbell and pounded on the door until Priscilla replied.

"Who's that?" the girl called through the locked door.

"This is Mrs. Thompson, open the door, honey." Mrs. Thompson was careful not to scare the child.

"No. My mommy says I mustn't open the door to anybody."

"But Priscilla, I think there's a fire in your house."

...cess to ...e roof and ...en to go below the height of the flames. He could not do so while carrying the dead-weight of the helpless 115-pound woman.

Then he saw another fireman, Mike Mays, motioning to him with his arms held out. Mays was on the roof of the next building, which was level with the fire escape. A space of only four feet separated the two buildings, but there was a fifty-foot drop to the ground. Lane tried to pass Mrs. Rogers over to Mays, but the gap was too wide.

Then the two men decided that the only chance to save the woman was to try something very dangerous. Lane reached back and threw Mrs. Rogers across the space between the buildings. For a moment the woman was not supported above the ground. Then Mays caught her by the neck and shoulders, and pulled her safely onto the roof. Mrs. Rogers was uninjured.

Lane then climbed to the roof of the burning building, went down another fire escape and back to fighting the fire.

---NEWSDAY
(Long Island, N.Y.)

Mosquitoes

...one night... musical instrumen... the same time. He made... dream come true. Today he... a brilliant musician with a ta... ent so real few people can be... lieve it.

When he blows one hor... (for example, the tenor saxophone), he is the equal of an... musician around today. Whe... he blows three horns at th... same time, he is truly out o... this world.

Kirk is a one-man band, th... master of forty-five music... instruments. Even more amaz... ing, he has been blind sinc... the age of two.

Kirk's regular instrumen... are the saxophone, the man... zello and the stritch (both o... which look like very long sax... ophones), and the flute. Whe... he plays, he keeps the fir... three around his neck and th... flute in the bell of his sa... Within arm's reach are also... one-foot siren, a cigar-shape... song flute---and a humming... box that he calls "The Ev... Box."

In the middle of the flut... solo, he may reach for th... song flute and play a due... using both his nose and hi... mouth. This is impossible t... most musicians, but Kirk, wh... has made a study of breat... control, can do it. He ha... learned to use his lungs t... capacity and to store air in hi... cheeks.

Kirk discovered the mag...

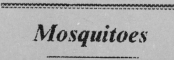

IMPROVING YOUR VOCABULARY

Here is a review of the words you learned in the first fifteen lessons. Choose the correct meaning of each word.

1. appeared   (a) made up one's mind; (b) saved; (c) looked like

2. area   (a) neighborhood; (b) amount of heat; (c) sport

3. attached   (a) found out; (b) fought; (c) joined

4. attention   (a) care and thought; (b) idea; (c) test to find something out

5. average   (a) not safe; (b) uneven; (c) like most others

6. battle   (a) fight; (b) save; (c) be happy with

7. captured   (a) found; (b) took prisoner; (c) moved slowly on hands and knees

8. common   (a) often met with; (b) strange; (c) not letting air in or out

9. completely   (a) at last; (b) totally; (c) dangerously

10. continue   (a) look at closely; (b) fix; (c) keep on

11. customer   (a) person who paints pictures; (b) person who goes to little-known places; (c) person who buys

12. damp   (a) a little wet; (b) not seen before; (c) easy

13. dangerous   (a) uneven; (b) common; (c) not safe

14. decided   (a) joined; (b) made up one's mind; (c) killed

15. destroyed   (a) killed; (b) choked; (c) kept on

16. disagree   (a) get together; (b) find out; (c) have different ideas

17. discovered   (a) hid; (b) found out for the first time; (c) saved

18. enjoy   (a) be happy with; (b) see in one's mind; (c) find fault with

19. entered   (a) joined; (b) went into; (c) made ready

20. examined   (a) looked at closely; (b) brought to life; (c) took prisoner

21. experiment   (a) space between two places; (b) person who looks into a problem carefully; (c) test to find something out

22. explorer   (a) person who goes to little-known places; (b) person who works a machine; (c) person who gets news for a newspaper

23. finally   (a) truly; (b) at last; (c) most of the time

24. fractured   (a) broke; (b) saw; (c) kept on

25. imagined   (a) looked like; (b) hit with force; (c) saw in the mind

26. mysterious   (a) worked by a machine; (b) often met with; (c) strange

27. narrow   (a) mean; (b) not wide; (c) like most others

28. noticed   (a) saw; (b) went into; (c) saved

29. often   (a) at some time; (b) at last; (c) many times

30. prepare   (a) be happy with; (b) make ready; (c) get

31. probably   (a) more likely than not; (b) totally; (c) over and over again

32. received   (a) told; (b) made up one's mind; (c) got

33. released   (a) got; (b) looked like; (c) let out

34. repair   (a) bring to life; (b) fix; (c) make ready

35. repeat   (a) brought forward; (b) finish; (c) do again

36. reported   (a) looked like; (b) told; (c) saw in the mind

37. rescued   (a) saved; (b) captured; (c) looked at closely

38. revived   (a) brought to life; (b) found out; (c) had different ideas

39. schedule   (a) amount of heat; (b) plan; (c) time of being free from school or work

40. scolded   (a) broke; (b) choked; (c) found fault with

41. several   (a) like most others; (b) more than one; (c) not even

42. silence   (a) no sound; (b) spot; (c) space between two places

43. supplies   (a) airplanes going to outer space; (b) things needed; (c) places where soldiers stay

44. surprise   (a) striking with the open hand; (b) something not expected; (c) try

45. temperature   (a) amount of heat; (b) plan; (c) outside

46. trapped   (a) said further; (b) hit with force; (c) caught without a way of getting out

47. trouble   (a) difficulty; (b) no sound; (c) laugh in a silly way

48. useless   (a) not letting air in or out; (b) not safe; (c) without success

49. usually   (a) dangerously; (b) most of the time; (c) totally

50. vacation   (a) care and thought; (b) time of being free from school or work; (c) test to find something out

---

WORD BUILDING

Match the word in column B to the proper word-building part in column A.

A	B
1. *ous* (as in danger*ous*)	(a) not
2. *un* (as in *un*happy)	(b) back; again

3. *er, or* (as in work*er*)   (c) together; with
4. *re* (as in *re*turn)   (d) having to do with
5. *con* (as in *con*duct)   (e) full of
6. *in* (as in *in*doors)   (f) measure
7. *port* (as in *port*able)   (g) a person who
8. *meter* (as in   (h) state of being
   speedo*meter*)   (i) into; not
9. *al* (as in music*al*)   (j) carry
10. *ness* (as in kind*ness*)

A Little Harder: Pick out the correct meaning of each of these words.

1. construct   (a) take away; (b) build; (c) return
2. contain   (a) hold; (b) be sad about; (c) reach for
3. courageous   (a) brave; (b) open; (c) quick
4. disappear   (a) come into sight; (b) become better; (c) not be seen any more
5. discontinue   (a) begin again; (b) stop; (c) try harder
6. disease   (a) rest; (b) hard work; (c) illness
7. disobey   (a) not listen to; (b) pay attention to; (c) stop
8. famous   (a) funny; (b) hurt; (c) very well-known
9. grateful   (a) very large; (b) thankful; (c) sad
10. humorous   (a) funny; (b) running; (c) important

11. inhale (a) put air into; (b) breathe out; (c) breathe in

12. melodious (a) not easy; (b) sweet-sounding; (c) angry

13. mental (a) having to do with the mind; (b) something difficult to repair; (c) easily found

14. plentiful (a) sad-sounding; (b) not enough; (c) more than enough

15. sorrowful (a) happy; (b) waiting; (c) unhappy

16. spacious (a) large; (b) well-known; (c) mean

17. thermometer (a) measure of air pressure; (b) measure of heat; (c) hot and cold

18. unemployed (a) hard-working; (b) foolish; (c) not working

19. uninjured (a) not hurt; (b) happy; (c) careful

20. watchful (a) wasting time; (b) careful; (c) more than enough

16. SEEING IS BELIEVING

DID YOU EVER HAVE TROUBLE CONVINCING SOMEONE OF THE TRUTH?

WOULD YOU HAVE BELIEVED JOHN ROBERTSON'S STORY?

LAKELAND, Fla., Dec. 16 (AP) — What would you do if you saw a sports car *traveling* at seventy miles an hour with a monkey at the wheel? The average *motorist* might think it best to say nothing — and try to forget it.

John Robertson had this *experience* yesterday on Interstate Highway 4 and decided to tell his story to the Highway Patrol. It took a lot of *convincing,* but the patrol office here finally decided to check his story. They radioed the Tampa office to watch for a sports car driven by a monkey.

Later, two troopers *spotted* the car and stopped it. A chimpanzee was sitting in the driver's seat and steering the car. In the *passenger's* seat was Peter Roper of Tampa, a circus showman. Mr. Roper had trained the chimp to steer while he *operated* the gas and brake *pedals.*

Mr. Roper was charged with *reckless* driving and having no driver's *license.* No charges were made against the chimp.

— LAKELAND LEDGER

CHECK YOUR UNDERSTANDING

1. Another title that would best explain the main idea of this story is:
   (a) Driving a Sports Car
   (b) A Chimpanzee in the Driver's Seat
   (c) Reckless Driving
   (d) The Highway Patrol
2. When John Robertson told his story to the Highway Patrol, he was
   (a) believed immediately.
   (b) not believed at all.
   (c) sent to the Tampa office.
   (d) believed after a while.
3. The chimpanzee
   (a) was in the car alone.
   (b) was charged with reckless driving.

111

(c) was steering the car.

(d) fed the gas and operated the brake.

4. The author of this story is most likely a

(a) writer of fiction stories.

(b) reporter.

(c) highway patrolman.

(d) teacher.

REACHING OUT

1. A line in this story that is meant to make you laugh is

(a) "No charges were made against the chimp."

(b) "The patrol office . . . finally radioed the Tampa office."

(c) "Two troopers spotted the car and stopped it."

(d) "In the passenger seat was Peter Roper of Tampa."

2. In the second paragraph are the words, "the patrol office here." The word *here* means

(a) Tampa, Florida.

(b) Interstate Highway 4.

(c) New York City.

(d) Lakeland, Florida.

FIRST THINGS FIRST

Arrange these events in the order in which they happened.

1. Two troopers stopped the car.
2. Mr. Roper was charged with reckless driving.
3. John Robertson told the Highway Patrol he had seen a monkey driving a car.
4. Mr. Roper trained the chimpanzee to steer a car.
5. John Robertson saw a monkey driving a car.

IMPROVING YOUR VOCABULARY

In the first column below and on the next page are the ten words in italics from the story. Pick out the best "story" meaning of each of these words.

1. *traveling* fast — (a) running; (b) walking; (c) going

2. an average *motorist* — (a) driver of a car; (b) walker; (c) automobile

3. had an *experience* — (a) unusual happening; (b) monkey; (c) forgetting

4. took a lot of *convincing* — (a) making a great deal of noise; (b) driving great distances; (c) making a person feel sure

5. *spotted* the car — (a) painted; (b) saw; (c) dirtied

6. *passenger* in a car — (a) person who goes in a car with the driver; (b) driver of a car; (c) back of the car

7. *operated* the brake — (a) cut open; (b) jammed; (c) worked

8. on the gas *pedal* — (a) something near the door; (b) something worked

by foot; (c) something worked by hand

9. *reckless* driving   (a) unsafe; (b) funny; (c) fine

10. driver's *license*   (a) chance for escape; (b) knowing how to do well; (c) legal right to do something

---

WORD BUILDING

The word *interstate* in the story above means *between states*. An interstate highway is a highway that runs through several states.

The prefix *inter* has two meanings. Sometimes it means *between* or *among*; at other times it means *with one another*.

> Example: *interscholastic* means *between schools.*
> *interwoven* means *woven with one another.*

To Do: Write the meaning of each of these words that begin with the prefix *inter*. Use the form of the word that is in the parentheses.

1. international (nations)
2. interplanetary (planets)
3. interlock (lock)
4. interracial (races)
5. interchange (change)

A Little Harder: Match the meaning in column B to the proper *inter* word in column A.

A	B
1. *interrupt* a story	(a) visit and talk with
2. *interview* a famous	(b) time between periods
person	of action; a pause
3. an *intersection*	(c) middle; being between
4. in an *intermediate*	(d) break in on
group	(e) a crossing
5. *intermission* of a	
ball game	

EXPRESSING YOURSELF

1. Tell about animals you've seen or heard about that have been taught to do unusual things.

2. Do you think that Peter Roper should have been charged with reckless driving for allowing the chimpanzee to steer the car? Why, or why not?

3. Write a paragraph telling about some strange or funny sight you have seen.

4. Imagine that you are John Robertson and one of your classmates is a policeman. Act out the scene in which you try to convince him about the monkey, but he thinks you are drunk or "seeing things."

17. WHAT A TRAFFIC JAM!

WHAT WAS THE WORST TRAFFIC JAM YOU WERE EVER IN?

WAS IT AS BAD AS THIS ONE?

LOS ANGELES, June 12 (AP) — Two trucks *collided* on the busy San Bernardino Freeway yesterday. One truck was loaded with 3,700 chickens and the other truck with 47 *steers*.

"It was unbelievable," said police officer Joe

Ramos. "The animals were running down the freeway in both directions. The chickens were squawking all over the place." Some of the hens began laying eggs.

Most of the chickens were rounded up by police officers, but the steers ran off. *Volunteers* on horseback went *galloping* after them. The steers *stampeded* through the streets of three nearby towns.

One steer was roped and tied in the playground of a public school.

Another steer caused five *minor* accidents before it was killed in a head-on crash with a car.

Freeway *traffic* was backed up more than six miles. No *humans* were *injured,* but it was more than five hours before the traffic *jam* finally let up.

— DENVER POST

CHECK YOUR UNDERSTANDING

1. Another title that would best explain the main idea of this story is:
   - (a) Chickens and Steers Cause Traffic Tie-up
   - (b) Policeman Has Busy Day
   - (c) Five Minor Accidents on Freeway
   - (d) Steer Roped in Playground
2. The animals were running down the freeway because
   - (a) the chickens were squawking.
   - (b) it was unbelievable.
   - (c) two trucks collided.
   - (d) the truck with the chickens had too big a load.
3. Because the trucks collided,
   - (a) freeway traffic was backed up more than six miles.
   - (b) a number of people were killed.
   - (c) all of the chickens were lost.
   - (d) Joe Ramos lost his job.
4. The traffic jam let up
   - (a) after six hours.
   - (b) after a steer was killed.
   - (c) right after the trucks collided.
   - (d) after five hours.

REACHING OUT

1. The one thing that did *not* happen as a result of the trucks colliding was that
   - (a) some hens began laying eggs.

(b) a number of people were hurt.

(c) a steer caused five minor accidents.

(d) volunteers on horseback went galloping after the steers.

2. A sound that is *not* written about in this story is that of

(a) children screaming.

(b) chickens squawking.

(c) horses galloping.

(d) steers stampeding.

FIRST THINGS FIRST

Arrange these events in the order in which they happened.

1. The traffic jam finally let up after five hours.
2. Two trucks collided on the freeway.
3. Animals started running down the freeway.
4. A steer was roped and tied in a school playground.
5. Volunteers went riding after the steers.

GETTING THE PICTURE

How good is your imagination? Can you "see" the things that are happening in a story as you read? The story in this lesson has many "pictures" for your imagination.

On the next page, pick out the words in the second column that finish the picture started in the first column. The answer to the first one is (c), "The steers . . . stampeded through the streets."

A	B
1. The steers	(a) collided on the free-way.
2. Two trucks	
3. One steer	(b) laid eggs.
4. Freeway traffic	(c) stampeded through the streets.
5. Some of the hens	
	(d) was killed in a head-on crash with a car.
	(e) was backed up more than six miles.

IMPROVING YOUR VOCABULARY

In the first column below and on the next page are the ten words in italics from the story. Pick out the best "story" meaning of each of these words.

1. trucks *collided*   (a) raced along; (b) hit together with force; (c) just missed one another

2. *steers* ran off   (a) horses; (b) pigs; (c) male cattle

3. *volunteers* went   (a) people who help others by their own choice; (b) run-away animals; (c) horseback riders

4. *galloping* after   (a) cheering; (b) running very fast; (c) shouting and crying

5. steers *stampeded*   (a) rushed away in a group; (b) walked calmly; (c) tried to sneak through

6. *minor* accident   (a) terrible; (b) people who work in mines; (c) not serious

7. *traffic* backed up   (a) women who shop; (b) automobiles going along a road; (c) road signs

8. no *humans* there   (a) animals; (b) automobiles; (c) people

9. no one *injured*   (a) hurt; (b) unhappy; (c) late for an appointment

10. traffic *jam*   (a) fun on a holiday; (b) people or things very crowded together; (c) people watching the sights

---

WORD BUILDING

The word *unbelievable* in the story above means *not able to be believed.*

Whenever you see *able* or *ible* at the end of a word, it means *able to be.*

Example: *playable* means *able to be played.*

To Do: Write the meaning of each of these words ending in *able* or *ible.* Use the form of the word that is in the parentheses.

1. breakable (broken)
2. sinkable (sunk)
3. readable (read)
4. beatable (beaten)
5. touchable (touched)

More: You cannot add *able* or *ible* to some words and still have a word. For example, you

121

cannot add *able* to *low*, since there is no such word as *lowable*.

For each of the following words, write "yes" in your notebook if you can add *able* or *ible* to make a new word. Write "no" if you cannot.

6. laugh
7. kind
8. music
9. narrow
10. kiss

A Little Harder: Match the meaning in column B to the proper *able* or *ible* word in column A.

A	B
1. *terrible* storm	(a) able to be sold
2. *reasonable* answer	(b) unable to be stood or put up with
3. *unbearable* heat	
4. *understandable* language	(c) causing great fear; awful
5. *salable* plan	(d) something that makes sense
	(e) able to be known

EXPRESSING YOURSELF

1. Tell of an unusually wild and disorderly sight you have seen.
2. What do you think can be done to help solve the traffic problems of our cities and highways?
3. What is the main cause of traffic accidents? Can you think of some ways to prevent them?
4. Imagine you were in the schoolyard when one of the escaping steers was roped and tied. Write a humorous paragraph about what you saw.

18. THE BEAUTY-CONTEST WINNER WAS A SOLDIER

WHEN MOST BOYS REACH THE AGE OF EIGHTEEN, THEY ARE LIKELY TO BE DRAFTED INTO THE ARMY. SHOULD GIRLS BE DRAFTED TOO?

HOW DOES ALIZA SADEH FEEL ABOUT BEING A SOLDIER?

Aliza Sadeh, a 21-year-old redhead, is a beauty queen with lots of energy. She was Miss Israel and

123

represented her country in the Miss *Universe* Beauty *Contest.*

Before Aliza became Miss Israel, however, she was a soldier in her country's army. Later, she even gave up her crown to help *defend* her country. This happened when Israel became *involved* in a war with a number of Arab *nations.*

"Every girl must join the army when she reaches the age of eighteen," Miss Sadeh *explained.* "You go to high school and then, boom, you are in the army! You learn to shoot, to walk carrying a rifle, and to work long hours."

Israel's girls also learn, as Aliza Sadeh did, not to wear make-up or long hair and not to paint their nails. But Aliza tucked up her long red hair to fool the army.

The young people of her country are not *draft-dodgers,* she said. Everyone goes into the army. "No one tries very hard to stay out," she said. "A few get married at seventeen to keep out of the army, but very few."

Aliza thinks that her country is the most *modern* in the world. Girls wear the latest *fashions* and "the young people are always on the go."

— WASHINGTON POST

CHECK YOUR UNDERSTANDING

1. Another title that would best explain the main idea of this story is:
   (a) Girl Soldier of Israel
   (b) Beauty Contests

124

(c) Israel

(d) Keeping out of the Army

2. Aliza gave up her title of Miss Israel because she

(a) could only keep it for one year.

(b) lost it in the following contest.

(c) joined the army to help defend her country.

(d) didn't want to wear long hair.

3. Most Israeli girls

(a) do not go into the army.

(b) try to stay out of the army.

(c) are beauty-contest winners.

(d) join the army at the age of eighteen.

4. Aliza is now

(a) married.

(b) Miss Israel.

(c) a high school student.

(d) a 21-year-old redhead.

5. Aliza thinks her country is

(a) old-fashioned.

(b) up-to-date.

(c) not worth fighting for.

(d) too modern.

REACHING OUT

1. Israeli girls in the army do *not*

(a) learn to fire a rifle.

(b) wear make-up.

(c) work long hours.

(d) march with a rifle.

2. Of the following, the words which are *not* the *exact* words spoken by Aliza Sadeh are:

(a) the girls wear the latest fashions.

125

(b) every girl must join the army when she reaches the age of eighteen.

(c) the young people are always on the go.

(d) you learn to work long hours.

PUTTING THE PIECES TOGETHER

Below is a title for each of the six paragraphs in the story. Put these titles in the order in which the paragraphs appeared in the story. The first one is done for you.

1. Aliza Helps Defend Her Country
2. Rules for the Appearance of Israel's Girl Soldiers
3. Aliza's Opinion of Her Country
4. What Girls Learn to Do in the Israeli Army
5. What Young People Think of the Draft in Israel
6. Aliza Sadeh as a Beauty Queen — Paragraph 1

IMPROVING YOUR VOCABULARY

In the first column below and on the next page are the ten words in italics from the story. Pick out the best "story" meaning of each of these words.

1. *represented* her country   (a) acted as an example; (b) showed films of; (c) was a soldier for

2. the entire *universe*   (a) country; (b) city; (c) world

3. a beauty *contest*   (a) trial of skill to see who will win; (b) quiz program; (c) means of deciding the future

4. *defend* her country   (a) defeat; (b) keep from harm; (c) run away from

5. became *involved*   (a) lost; (b) took part in; (c) fought to the finish

6. a number of *nations*   (a) cities; (b) people from other lands; (c) countries

7. she *explained*   (a) complained; (b) gave reasons for; (c) laughed loudly

8. *draft-dodgers*   (a) people who catch cold easily; (b) people who try to keep from going into the army; (c) people who run away from trouble

9. *modern* country   (a) old-fashioned; (b) up-to-date; (c) new

10. latest *fashions*   (a) hats; (b) clothing styles; (c) news of the world

---

WORD BUILDING

The word *defend* in the story above means *keep from harm or danger.*

Explanation: The prefix *de* means *down* or *from.* The stem *fend* means *strike. Defend* then means to strike down or away from you those who are trying to cause harm; therefore, *keep from harm.*

127

When you see *de* at the start of a word, it will almost always mean *down* or *from*.

Example: *demote* means *to move down in grade or rank*. A soldier who is demoted has a lower rank than he once had.

To Do: Match the meaning in column B to the proper *de* word in column A.

A	B
1. *descend* the stairs	(a) put down
2. *decline* an invitation to a party	(b) make less
	(c) go down
3. *describe* what you saw	(d) write down, or tell
4. *deposit* money in a bank	(e) turn down
5. *decrease* in payment	

A Little Harder: Match the meaning in column B to the proper *de* word in column A.

A	B
1. *decide* where to go	(a) take away
2. *deduct* for taxes	(b) put off
3. *delay* leaving	(c) leave
4. take a *detour*	(d) make up one's mind
5. *depart* early	(e) roundabout way

EXPRESSING YOURSELF

1. Write a paragraph telling whether you think girls should be drafted into the United States Army.

2. Is the draft the best way of getting soldiers for our country's army? Can you suggest any better ways? Is the present way of drafting men fair?
3. Do you think it was wrong of Aliza Sadeh to disobey her army orders and hide her long hair? Why?
4. Aliza thinks her country is the most modern in the world. Two reasons she gives are that the girls wear the latest fashions and the young people are always on the go. What three reasons might you give to show that a country is modern? What three reasons might you give to show that a country is old-fashioned?

19. FIGHTING WITH SHARKS

SHARKS HAVE LONG BEEN FEARED BY SWIMMERS AND DIVERS.

WHAT DOES THIS STORY TELL YOU TO DO IF YOU EVER MEET A SHARK FACE TO FACE?

Most sharks are dangerous. The largest kind of shark — the whale shark — has small teeth and is quite *harmless* to people. However, blue sharks, tiger sharks, white sharks and hammerheads are *enemies* of man.

Man-eaters are always a danger to swimmers in shark waters. Sometimes, though, men have used strange methods when they're suddenly faced with a shark.

During World War II, soldiers and sailors whose boats or planes were destroyed drifted helplessly on the ocean in small rafts. While waiting to be saved, the men had to *struggle* to stay alive and were often *attacked* by sharks. In some cases, they had few weapons to protect themselves with. They found that just splashing water seemed to help keep the sharks away.

One sailor was swimming for his life in the Atlantic Ocean after his boat had been blown up. He saw a shark swimming toward him. He hit the shark several times with his bare fist, and that drove it off!

Once, in Australia, a fisherman was fishing after sunset. He hooked a big fish and drew it towards the shore. His line broke when the fish was

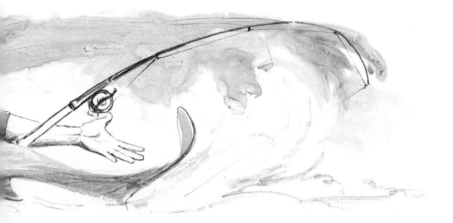

only a few yards from shore. The fisherman waded into the water to try to capture it with his hands. In the *dim* light, it looked like the kind of fish that could be *handled* without danger.

He put his arms around the fish and *wrestled* with it. Dragging it to the beach turned out to be harder than he had *expected,* but at last he pulled it in. When he turned a light on it, he was *amazed.* He had caught a shark! It was small for a shark, but it was the man-eating *type* and was about as long as a man is tall.

All in all, the best way to handle sharks is to keep far away from them.

— "Ask Uncle Ray," ST. LOUIS POST-DISPATCH

CHECK YOUR UNDERSTANDING

1. Another title that would best explain the main idea of this story is:
   (a) Wrestling a Shark
   (b) Sharks
   (c) The Second World War
   (d) People Against Sharks
2. The shark that is least dangerous to man is the
   (a) white shark
   (b) whale shark.
   (c) tiger shark.
   (d) hammerhead shark.
3. Soldiers and sailors in the Second World War found that they could sometimes drive sharks away by
   (a) splashing water.

(b) swimming.

(c) getting on a raft.

(d) fishing.

4. This story tells you that sharks are usually

(a) friendly.

(b) small.

(c) afraid of people.

(d) dangerous.

5. After the Australian fisherman found he had caught a shark, he was

(a) frightened.

(b) surprised.

(c) unhappy.

(d) angry.

REACHING OUT

1. This story tells you that the best way to handle sharks is to

(a) hit them with your fist.

(b) keep far away from them.

(c) splash water.

(d) wrestle with them.

2. The shark the fisherman caught was *not*

(a) small as sharks go.

(b) a man-eating type.

(c) a harmless fish.

(d) about as long as a man is tall.

FIRST THINGS FIRST

Arrange these things in the order in which they happened to the fisherman.

133

1. He got the fish to the beach.
2. He hooked a big fish.
3. His line broke.
4. He found he had caught a shark.
5. He wrestled with the fish.
6. He waded into the water to get the fish.

WHAT'S THE REASON?

When you read you sometimes have to be a good detective. You have to discover *why* things happen. See if you can pick out the "why" of these questions.

1. The whale shark is harmless because he
   (a) has small teeth.
   (b) is very large.
   (c) is friendly.
   (d) has a hammerhead.
2. Soldiers and sailors in the Second World War were on small rafts in the ocean because
   (a) they were looking for sharks.
   (b) their boats or planes had been destroyed.
   (c) they were fishing.
   (d) they were going swimming.
3. The fisherman wrestled with the shark because
   (a) he had wrestled sharks before.
   (b) he thought it was a fish that could be handled safely.
   (c) it was not a man-eating shark.
   (d) he wanted to show that he could fight a shark.

134

4. The fisherman couldn't tell he had a shark because
   (a) the light was dim.
   (b) he didn't know what sharks looked like.
   (c) his line broke.
   (d) he was wading.
5. The fisherman waded into the water to catch the fish because
   (a) his line broke.
   (b) he liked to wrestle with fish.
   (c) he knew it was a shark.
   (d) that is the way Australians catch fish.

IMPROVING YOUR VOCABULARY

In the first column below and on the next page are the ten words in italics from the story. Pick out the best "story" meaning of each of these words.

1. *harmless* to people — (a) safe; (b) dangerous; (c) important

2. *enemies* of people — (a) not friends; (b) cousins; (c) friends

3. *struggle* to stay alive — (a) swim; (b) walk a long distance; (c) work hard against great difficulties

4. sharks *attacked* — (a) seen from a distance; (b) set out to hurt; (c) joined to

5. *dim* light — (a) bright; (b) badly done; (c) not bright

135

6. *handled* the fish	(a) dealt with; (b) caught; (c) put in a sack
7. *wrestled* with it	(a) talked; (b) fought; (c) played
8. more than he *expected*	(a) thought something would happen; (b) was able to do something; (c) was willing to allow
9. was *amazed*	(a) sorry; (b) happy; (c) greatly surprised
10. man-eating *type*	(a) kind; (b) shark; (c) fish

WORD BUILDING

The word *harmless* in the story above means *without harm;* therefore, *safe.*

When you see *less* at the end of a word, it means *without.*

Example: *coatless* means *without a coat.*

To Do: Write the meaning of each of these words ending in *less* in your notebook.

> **1.** careless
> **2.** joyless
> **3.** nameless
> **4.** meatless
> **5.** endless

A Little Harder: You cannot add *less* to some words and still have a word. For example, you cannot add *less* to *brave* since there is no such word as *braveless.*

For each of the following words, write "yes"

in your notebook if you can add *less* and make a
correct new word. Write "no" if you cannot.

1. good
2. hat
3. pain
4. off
5. poor

EXPRESSING YOURSELF

1. Tell of dangerous occupations some men have.
2. Tell a story you have heard about sharks.
3. Do you like to fish? Write a paragraph telling
   why.
4. Imagine you were lost and alone on a small raft
   in the ocean. Write a paragraph or two telling
   what you could do to stay alive, what you might
   see and what you might think about.

20. THE POLICEMAN-ARTIST

WHEN IT IS TIME FOR YOU TO DECIDE ON AN OCCUPATION, WHAT WILL YOU LOOK FOR? WHAT, BESIDES MONEY, IS IMPORTANT TO YOU?

WHY IS OTIS RATHEL HAPPY WITH HIS JOB?

For more than four months a mysterious criminal robbed and *terrorized* a *section* of Chicago.

One night a 25-year-old man was arrested on a minor charge. Policemen noticed the man's *resemblance* to a drawing of the mystery bandit done by an artist. They called in *witnesses*. Hours later they knew they had finally captured their mystery bandit.

Otis Rathel was the artist who drew the *sketch* that helped capture the bandit. He is also a policeman. When he makes a sketch, he first listens to witnesses *describe* a criminal. Then he draws the criminal. His drawings have led to dozens of arrests.

Rathel never went to art school. He taught himself to draw. He was a commercial artist for a business firm before joining the police force. Then he worked for ten years on the narcotics squad before moving on to his *present* job. The narcotics squad is a police group that watches for the illegal use of drugs.

He was once *featured* on the television show, "I've Got a Secret." He says the hardest part of his job is to draw the shape of the face. After that, the rest comes easier.

Witnesses are often nervous, but Rathel puts them at *ease*. Women are better at describing men, while men are better at describing women. But, he says, children are the best witnesses of all. They know *exactly* what they have seen and won't rest a minute until you've sketched it.

— EBONY

CHECK YOUR UNDERSTANDING

1. Another title that would best explain the main idea of this story is:
   (a) His Drawings Capture Criminals
   (b) A Mysterious Crime

(c) Nervous Witnesses

(d) Teaching Yourself to Draw

2. The mystery bandit was captured because

(a) he was arrested for attacking a police officer.

(b) he was immediately recognized.

(c) he resembled the sketch drawn by Otis Rathel.

(d) policemen surrounded him.

3. Rathel

(a) went to art school.

(b) is not a police officer.

(c) went straight from college to the police force.

(d) taught himself to draw.

4. According to Rathel, the best witnesses are

(a) nervous.

(b) children.

(c) men.

(d) women.

5. Rathel's drawings of criminals

(a) are done on his spare time.

(b) have led to no arrests.

(c) have led to dozens of arrests.

(d) have led to about ten arrests.

REACHING OUT

1. Otis Rathel was featured on a television show probably because

(a) he never went to art school.

(b) he puts witnesses at ease.

(c) he has an unusual job.

(d) he was on the narcotics squad.

2. The statement below that is *not* true is:
   (a) Rathel says that the hardest part of his job is getting the shape of the face right.
   (b) Women describe other women better than they describe men.
   (c) Rathel draws criminals by listening to the descriptions of witnesses.
   (d) Rathel worked on the narcotics squad for ten years.

FIRST THINGS FIRST

Arrange these events in the order in which they happened.

1. Otis Rathel drew a sketch of the mystery bandit.
2. The mystery bandit was arrested on a minor charge.
3. A mystery bandit terrorized Chicago for four months.
4. Police finally knew they had captured the mystery bandit.
5. Police noticed the resemblance of the man they had arrested to the mystery bandit as sketched by Rathel.
6. Witnesses identified the arrested man as the mystery bandit.

IMPROVING YOUR VOCABULARY

In the first column on the next page are the ten words in italics from the story. Pick out the best "story" meaning of each of these words.

1. *terrorized* the city
(a) caused great fear; (b) walked around in; (c) found out about

2. *section* of the city
(a) house; (b) weakness; (c) part

3. *resemblance* to the bandit
(a) kindness; (b) running away; (c) likeness

4. *witnesses* to the crime
(a) pictures; (b) people who saw something happen; (c) people who helped a criminal escape

5. drew the *sketch*
(a) gun; (b) rough drawing; (c) person charged with a crime

6. *describe* the person
(a) tell in words how something looks; (b) capture; (c) try to bring back

7. in the *present*
(a) past; (b) future; (c) at this time

8. *featured* on the show
(a) listening closely to; (b) put in a position of importance; (c) known to many people

9. he felt at *ease*
(a) free from pain or trouble; (b) in a sitting position; (c) greatly troubled

10. know *exactly*
(a) something; (b) nothing; (c) without any error

WORD BUILDING

The word *describe* in the story above means *write or tell how something looks*. The prefix *de* means *down* and the stem *scrib* means write.

142

When you see *scrib* or *scrip* in a word, it has the meaning of *write*.

Example: The word *scribe* means a writer.

To Do: Match the meaning in column B to the proper *scrib* or *scrip* word in column A.

A	B
1. *scribble* a test answer	(a) the Bible
2. *prescribe* medicine	(b) agree to receive and pay for
3. *subscribe* to a magazine	(c) write carelessly
4. fine *script*	(d) advise as treatment for an illness
5. read *Scripture*	(e) handwriting

EXPRESSING YOURSELF

1. Would you like a job like Otis Rathel's? Why?
2. "I've Got a Secret" is a television show that presents people who have unusual secrets. If you were on the program, what would your secret be? Do you know someone who would be an interesting guest on the show? What would that person's secret be?
3. Write a paragraph telling about a job you would like to have when you leave school.
4. Write a letter applying for that job. Tell your qualifications for it.

REVIEW OF LESSONS 16-20

IMPROVING YOUR VOCABULARY

Choose the correct meaning of each of the words below. (The number in parentheses after each word is the number of the lesson where the word first appeared.)

1. amazed (19)   (a) greatly surprised; (b) dealt with; (c) acted as an example

2. attacked (19)   (a) rushed away in a group; (b) took part in; (c) set out to hurt

3. collided (17)   (a) hit together with force; (b) hurt; (c) fought

4. contest (18)   (a) legal right to do something; (b) trial of skill to

144

see who will win; (c) un-usual happening

5. convincing (16)   (a) going very fast; (b) taking part in; (c) making a person feel sure

6. defend (18)   (a) protect from harm; (b) work; (c) deal with

7. describe (20)   (a) put in a position of importance; (b) act as an example; (c) write or tell how something looks

8. dim (19)   (a) up-to-date; (b) sur-prised; (c) not bright

9. draft-dodgers (18)   (a) people who help others of their own choice; (b) automobiles going along a road; (c) people who try to keep from going into the army

10. ease (20)   (a) people or things very crowded together; (b) freedom from pain or trouble; (c) legal right to do something

11. enemies (19)   (a) not friends; (b) coun-tries; (c) male cattle

12. exactly (20)   (a) safely; (b) without any error; (c) easily

13. expected (19)   (a) thought something would happen; (b) worked; (c) rushed away in a group

14. experience (16)   (c) unusual happening; (b) likeness; (c) trial of skill to see who will win

145

15. explained (18) (a) caused great fear; (b) put in a position of importance; (c) gave reasons for

16. fashions (18) (a) rough drawings; (b) legal rights to do something; (c) clothing styles

17. featured (20) (a) acted as an example; (b) put in a position of importance; (c) told in words how something looked

18. galloping (17) (a) going very fast; (b) working hard against great difficulties; (c) fighting

19. handled (19) (a) gave reasons for; (b) saw; (c) dealt with

20. harmless (19) (a) safe; (b) not bright; (c) unsafe

21. humans (17) (a) people who help others by their own choice; (b) countries; (c) people

22. injured (17) (a) caused great fear; (b) hurt; (c) dealt with

23. involved (18) (a) fought; (b) took part in; (c) thought something would happen

24. jam (17) (a) people or things very crowded together; (b) automobiles going along a road; (c) unusual happening

25. license (16) (a) trial of skill to see

who will win; (b) clothing style; (c) a legal right to do something

26. minor (17)　　　(a) up-to-date; (b) unsafe; (c) not serious

27. modern (18)　　(a) not bright; (b) up-to-date; (c) surprised

28. motorist (16)　　(a) driver of a car; (b) automobile; (c) person who saw something happen

29. nations (18)　　(a) countries; (b) not friends; (c) parts

30. operated (16)　　(a) gave reasons for; (b) acted as an example; (c) worked

31. passenger (16)　　(a) something worked by foot; (b) person who goes in a car with the driver; (c) driver of a car

32. pedal (16)　　　(a) male cattle; (b) something worked by foot; (c) machine

33. present (20)　　(a) at this time; (b) clothing style; (c) freedom from pain or trouble

34. reckless (16)　　(a) easy; (b) surprising; (c) unsafe

35. represented (18)　　(a) hurt; (b) acted as an example; (c) thought something would happen

36. resemblance (20　　(a) unusual happening; (b) legal right to do something; (c) likeness

147

37. section (20) (a) part; (b) kind; (c) world

38. sketch (20) (a) rough drawing; (b) people or things very crowded together; (c) something worked by foot

39. (spotted (16) (a) caused great fear; (b) gave reasons for; (c) saw

40. stampeded (17) (a) fought; (b) put in a position of importance; (c) rushed away in a group

41. steers (17) (a) clothing styles; (b) male cattle; (c) drivers of cars

42. struggle (19) (a) go; (b) work hard against great difficulties; (c) give reasons for

43. terrorized (20) (a) caused great fear; (b) worked; (c) made a person feel sure

44. traffic (17) (a) people; (b) part; (c) automobiles going along a road

45. traveling (16) (a) going; (b) seeing something happen; (c) taking part in

46. type (19) (a) legal right to do something; (b) rough drawing; (c) kind

47. universe (18) (a) driver of a car; (b) part; (c) world

48. volunteers (17) (a) people who help others

148

by their own choice; (b) people who go in a car with the driver; (c) people who try to keep from going into the army

49. witnesses (20) (a) people who help others by their own choice; (b) people who saw something happen; (c) automobiles going along a road

50. wrestled (19) (a) went very fast; (b) worked; (c) fought

WORD BUILDING

Match the meaning in column B to the proper word-building part in column A.

A	B
1. *scrib, scrip* (20)	(a) down; from
2. *inter* (16)	(b) write
3. *able, ible* (17)	(c) without
4. *less* (19)	(d) between; among; with one another
5. *de* (18)	(e) able to be

A Little Harder: Match the meaning in column B to the proper word in column A.

A	B
1. unbearable (17)	(a) make up one's mind
2. depart (18)	(b) unable to be stood or put up with
3. interrupt (16)	

4. decide (18)
5. scribble (20)
6. deduct (18)
7. interview (16)
8. subscribe (20)
9. intermission (16)
10. delay (18)

(c) write carelessly
(d) time between periods of action; a pause
(e) take away
(f) break in on
(g) leave
(h) put off
(i) agree to receive and pay for
(j) visit and talk with

21. NERVOUS MINUTES

ARE THERE TIMES WHEN A CHILD SHOULD NOT OBEY HIS PARENTS?

DECIDE WHETHER PRISCILLA BROWN WAS *TOO* OBEDIENT.

Priscilla Brown is a very good child. She is only six years old but is *responsible* and *obedient*. She takes *excellent* care of her four younger brothers and never *disobeys* her mother. Since yesterday, however, Mrs. Mary Brown, her mother, probably thinks she is a little too obedient.

The Browns live on the third floor of an apartment house in Brooklyn. Roderick Thompson, four years old, lives in an *adjoining* apartment. At 9 A.M. yesterday, Roderick noticed smoke *curling* from under the Browns' door. He called his mother, Mrs. Sophie Thompson, who rang the doorbell and *pounded* on the door until Priscilla *replied*.

"Who's that?" the girl called through the locked door.

"This is Mrs. Thompson. Open the door, honey." Mrs. Thompson was careful not to *alarm* the child.

"No. My mommy says I mustn't open the door to anybody."

"But Priscilla, I think there's a fire in your house."

"I know there is. My brother Tommy set the fire."

"Priscilla! Call your mother quickly!"

"She's not here."

"Where is she?"

"In the cellar washing clothes."

After ten *tense* minutes, Priscilla was talked into opening the door. Mrs. Thompson and her neighbors rushed into the smoky apartment and carried out six children: Priscilla and her brothers, Tommy, five; Donald, four; Louis, three; and Theodore, eight months; and two-year-old Ronald Lewis, a neighbor's boy. The children were crying and coughing, but unhurt.

— NEW YORK TIMES

CHECK YOUR UNDERSTANDING

1. Another title that would best explain the main idea of this story is:
   (a) Fire!
   (b) A Disobedient Girl
   (c) Obedience Carried Too Far
   (d) A Narrow Escape
2. Priscilla did not open the door because
   (a) her mother told her not to.
   (b) she did not know Mrs. Thompson.
   (c) she did not think there was a fire in the apartment.
   (d) her mother was washing clothes.
3. The fire was started by
   (a) Priscilla.
   (b) Roderick Thompson.
   (c) Mrs. Thompson.
   (d) Priscilla's oldest brother.
4. Priscilla can best be described as
   (a) disobedient.

(b) careless.

(c) obedient.

(d) lazy.

5. As the neighbors waited for Priscilla to open the door, they were

(a) calm.

(b) laughing.

(c) nervous.

(d) angry.

REACHING OUT

1. After the fire, the children were *not*

(a) crying.

(b) saved.

(c) hurt.

(d) coughing.

2. Who said, "In the cellar washing clothes"?

(a) Priscilla.

(b) Mrs. Thompson.

(c) Donald.

(d) Mrs. Brown.

FIRST THINGS FIRST

Arrange these events in the order in which they happened.

1. Priscilla refused to open the door for Mrs. Thompson.

2. The fire started.

3. Priscilla was talked into opening the door.

4. The children were carried out of the apartment.
5. The neighbors rushed into the smoky apartment.

IMPROVING YOUR VOCABULARY

In the first column below and on the next page are the ten words in italics from the story. Pick out the best "story" meaning of each of these words.

1. *responsible* girl — (a) careless; (b) childish; (c) able to be trusted
2. the child is *obedient* — (a) good at household duties; (b) does what he is told; (c) small in size
3. *excellent* care — (a) once in a while; (b) very, very good; (c) unwanted
4. *disobeys* her mother — (a) raises one's voice to; (b) listens closely to; (c) does not do what one is told to do
5. *adjoining* apartment — (a) next to; (b) end; (c) far off
6. smoke *curling* — (a) rising in rings; (b) smelling strongly; (c) looking black
7. *pounded* on the door — (a) tapped gently; (b) hit hard again and again; (c) leaned
8. Priscilla *replied* — (a) sang; (b) opened; (c) answered
9. did not *alarm* — (a) hit; (b) be good to; (c) fill with fear suddenly

10. *tense* minutes   (a) quick; (b) nervous; (c) more than ten

---

WORD BUILDING

The word *adjoining* in the story means *next to* or *close to*. The prefix *ad* at the start of a word almost always means *to* or *toward*.

Example: *advise* means *give an opinion to*.

To Do: Match the meaning in column B to the proper *ad* word in column A.

A	**B**
1. advance	(a) something that sticks to something else
2. address	
3. adhesive	(b) call public attention to
4. adjust	(c) fit to
5. advertise	(d) move toward
	(e) speak to

A Little Harder: In each of the following sentences, change the underlined words to one of the *ad* words from the first column above.

1. The President will *speak* to Congress.
2. The supermarket will *call public attention to* special sales every week.
3. This tape is *something that sticks to something else*.
4. The soldiers *move toward* the enemy.
5. A tailor will *fit* the pants *to* your body.

EXPRESSING YOURSELF

1. What kind of rules should a child be taught to obey? Why?
2. Are there things a child should decide for himself? How would you teach him to do so?
3. What safety measures do you and your family take to prevent fires?
4. Draw up a list of rules which a good baby-sitter should follow.
5. Write a paragraph telling the one thing you would take with you if there was a fire in your house, and why.

22. HE LOVES HIS COUNTRY

No. 103

June 6 19 68 1-12 / 210

PAY TO THE ORDER OF United States of America $ 1000.00/100

One Thousand and no — Dollars

FIDELITY BANK NORTHERN TRUST COMPANY

93511 SUTPHIN AVENUE
MILWAUKEE 54
WISC.

Gus Pappas

⑈0210⑈0210⑈ 051⑈212103⑈

ARE YOU GLAD YOU LIVE IN THE UNITED STATES AND NOT SOMEWHERE ELSE? WHY?

WHAT DO YOU THINK OF THE WAY GUS PAPPAS SHOWED HIS LOVE FOR HIS COUNTRY?

MILWAUKEE, Wisc., June 6 — A 78-year-old Greek *immigrant* mailed $1,000 to the United States government Tuesday because, he explained, "this country has been good to me."

Gus Pappas came to this country from Greece when he was 16 years old. When he *arrived* in the United States he had only the clothes on his back, a suitcase and much *faith* in the freedom and *opportunity* in the United States.

"When I married my wife here in America, we didn't have anything," Gus said. "I worked as a cook. When I saved $300, I quit. I borrowed some money. I bought my restaurant for $850. But, mister, within three months I was making a good living — and I got no help from anybody."

He is not *wealthy* now. The $1,000 is a large part of what he has left in the bank.

"I believe very much that where I eat my bread, I should love and *protect* and fight for," Mr. Pappas said. "This is my home."

Mr. Pappas is very *proud* that he won his United States *citizenship* by serving in the army during World War One.

He dropped his $1,000 check into a mailbox. With it was a note:

"Please *accept* this small amount in deep *appreciation* for the many happy years of my life spent as a citizen of this free and blessed country."

— MILWAUKEE JOURNAL

CHECK YOUR UNDERSTANDING

1. Another title that would best explain the main idea of this story is:
   (a) An Immigrant's Gift to His Country
   (b) The Hard Life of an Immigrant
   (c) A Man Who Made Good
   (d) Winning Citizenship Through Army Service

2. Gus Pappas mailed $1,000 to the United States government because
   (a) he felt the United States had been good to him.
   (b) he owed the money for taxes.
   (c) his conscience bothered him.
   (d) he had too much money in his bank account.
3. The $1,000 Gus sent to the government was
   (a) all the money he had.
   (b) a small part of his money.
   (c) a large part of what he had in the bank.
   (d) borrowed from a bank.
4. When a government worker received Gus's letter and check, he was most likely
   (a) unhappy.
   (b) surprised.
   (c) impatient.
   (d) angry.
5. Gus came to this country
   (a) seventy-eight years ago.
   (b) sixteen years ago.
   (c) more than seventy years ago.
   (d) more than sixty years ago.
6. When Gus married his wife, he had
   (a) $300.
   (b) $850.
   (c) a restaurant.
   (d) no money.
7. During World War One, Gus
   (a) came to the United States.
   (b) was in the army.
   (c) opened a restaurant.
   (d) got married.

REACHING OUT

1. Gus Pappas could best be described as
   (a) complaining.
   (b) lazy.
   (c) loyal.
   (d) selfish.
2. When Gus came to the United States, he did *not* have
   (a) faith in the United States.
   (b) a suitcase.
   (c) clothes on his back.
   (d) a job.
3. Gus is *not*
   (a) almost eighty years old.
   (b) a citizen of the United States.
   (c) rich.
   (d) a Greek immigrant.
4. To open his restaurant, Gus did *not*
   (a) save $300 working as a cook.
   (b) pay $850 for it.
   (c) borrow money.
   (d) get help from other people.

FIRST THINGS FIRST

Arrange these things in the order in which Gus Pappas did them.
1. He saved $300 working as a cook.
2. He came to the United States from Greece.
3. He mailed a $1,000 check to the United States government.

161

4. He got married.

5. He opened a restaurant.

IMPROVING YOUR VOCABULARY

In the first column below and on the next page are the ten words in italics from the story. Pick out the best "story" meaning of each of these words.

1. Greek *immigrant*   (a) person who has worked hard all his life; (b) person who comes from one country to another to live; (c) person who spends his life doing good deeds

2. he *arrived*   (a) went away; (b) went back to; (c) came to

3. *faith* in freedom   (a) anger at; (b) trust; (c) money

4. found *opportunity*   (a) good chance; (b) hardship; (c) life

5. not *wealthy*   (a) old; (b) poor; (c) rich

6. *protect* his home   (a) keep from harm; (b) talk about; (c) run from

7. very *proud*   (a) be unhappy about; (b) quick to remember; (c) thinking well of oneself

162

8. enjoyed *citizenship*   (a) prize for serving one's country; (b) being a member of a country; (c) medal for bravery

9. please *accept*   (a) give back; (b) take unwillingly; (c) spend

10. deep *appreciation*   (a) pain; (b) memory; (c) thankfulness

---

WORD BUILDING

The word *protect* in the story above means *keep from harm.* It is built up from two parts: *tect,* meaning *cover,* and *pro,* meaning *in front of.* When you protect yourself in a fight, you cover the front of your body.

The prefix *pro* means *in front of, before* and *forward.*

Example: *progress* means *moving forward.*

To Do: Match the meaning in column B to the proper *pro* word in column A.

A	**B**
1. *proceed* with the game	(a) drive forward
2. a movie *projector*	(b) moving forward in rank or importance
3. *promotion* on the job	(c) put forward; suggest
4. *propel* the bullet	(d) machine that throws pictures forward on a screen
5. *propose* a plan	(e) go forward

EXPRESSING YOURSELF

1. "It was foolish for Gus Pappas to give almost all his savings to the United States government." Do you agree or disagree? Why?
2. Tell of some immigrant you know. Why did he leave the country of his birth? How wise was he to do so?
3. Write a paragraph telling of some person who started with very little, and through hard work, became successful.
4. Imagine that you are the government worker who received the letter. Write a letter to Mr. Pappas telling him what you think of his gift.

23. MOSQUITOES

OUCH! DO YOU SEEM TO GET BITTEN BY MOSQUITOES MORE OFTEN THAN ANYONE ELSE DOES?

HERE ARE SOME USEFUL CLUES ON HOW TO HELP KEEP MOSQUITOES AWAY!

Some people *attract* twice as many mosquitoes as others do. How come?

Mosquitoes "go for" dark-skinned, warm-skinned and healthy people, say *experts* who have studied them.

Mosquitoes also choose people who sweat a great deal, breathe heavily, jump around a lot or use perfume. They also love people in dark clothing.

Clearly, then, to *avoid* bites you should dress in light-colored clothing, bathe *frequently,* be quiet and avoid the use of perfume.

There are some 2,500 kinds of mosquitoes in the world. Some are more vicious than others and some even cause *disease.* Among the diseases spread by mosquitoes are malaria and yellow fever.

Most mosquitoes you meet just cause a sore, *swollen* and itchy spot. This happens because when they bite, they *inject* a little *saliva* into you. It is the *female* mosquito that usually does the biting.

Mosquitoes don't live very long. They are not likely, in their short lives, to travel more than three blocks away from the place where they were born. The mosquito that bites you may have grown up in some still water in the gutters along your roof. If all places where water settles were cleared, mosquitoes would not be able to grow.

Until then, your drug store will have many kinds of mosquito *repellent* you can rub on to help keep them away.

— NEWSDAY (Long Island, N.Y.)

CHECK YOUR UNDERSTANDING

1. Another title that would best explain the main idea of this story is:
   (a) Some Facts About Mosquitoes
   (b) 2,500 Kinds of Mosquitoes
   (c) Mosquito Repellent
   (d) Watch Out for the Female Mosquito
2. To keep from being bitten by mosquitoes, you should

(a) wear dark clothing.
(b) use perfume.
(c) bathe often.
(d) breathe heavily.

3. All mosquitoes
   (a) need still water to grow in.
   (b) cause disease.
   (c) are females.
   (d) are of the same kind.

4. A mosquito bite makes a sore and swollen spot because
   (a) mosquitoes spread disease.
   (b) the mosquito grows in water.
   (c) mosquitoes inject a little saliva into you.
   (d) mosquitoes have repellent.

5. Mosquitoes
   (a) grow best in a dry climate.
   (b) always live in gutters.
   (c) travel great distances from where they are born.
   (d) have short lives.

WHAT'S THE WRONG ANSWER?

In the following questions, three answers are right and one is wrong. Pick out the *wrong* answer.

1. Mosquitoes like
   (a) dark-skinned people.
   (b) sick people.
   (c) people who sweat a lot.
   (d) people who use perfume.

167

2. A mosquito bite leaves a spot that is
  (a) itchy.
  (b) perfumed.
  (c) sore.
  (d) swollen.
3. Mosquitoes
  (a) cause disease.
  (b) spread malaria.
  (c) bite.
  (d) like to bite quiet people.
4. Mosquitoes
  (a) grow in still water.
  (b) don't travel far.
  (c) grow only in places close to the ground.
  (d) have short lives.

PUTTING THE PIECES TOGETHER

This story can be divided into five main ideas or topics. Below is a title for each of these topics. Put the titles in the order in which the topics appeared in the story. The first one is done for you.
  1. People Mosquitoes Like—Topic 1
  2. How to Avoid Mosquito Bites
  3. Why the Mosquito Bite is Sore and Itchy
  4. Where Mosquitoes Grow
  5. Diseases Caused by Mosquitoes

IMPROVING YOUR VOCABULARY

In the first column on the next page are the

168

ten words in italics from the story. Pick out the best "story" meaning of each of these words.

1. *attract* mosquitoes — (a) draw to oneself; (b) bite; (c) drive away

2. *experts* have found — (a) people who get bitten; (b) people who wait; (c) people who know a lot about some special thing.

3. *avoid* bites — (a) go out and get; (b) keep away from; (c) invite

4. bathe *frequently* — (a) seldom; (b) often; (c) less and less

5. cause *disease* — (a) illness; (b) unhappiness; (c) death

6. *female* mosquito — (a) the man in the family; (b) the vicious kind; (c) the sex that brings forth young

7. *swollen* spot — (a) red; (b) colorful; (c) larger than usual

8. *inject* something — (a) force into; (b) take away; (c) put back

9. a little *saliva* — (a) bite; (b) the liquid in the mouth; (c) illness

10. mosquito *repellent* — (a) something that will help mosquitoes grow; (b) something that will tell you about a subject; (c) something used to keep insects away

WORD BUILDING

The word *inject* in the story above means *force into.* As you learned in Lesson 13, *in* means *into.* The stem *ject* means throw. Sometimes it means *force,* as in *inject.*

Example: A *projector* is *a machine that throws pictures forward on a screen.*

To Do: Match the meaning in column B to the proper *ject* word in column A.

A	B
1. *rejected* by the army	(a) be against; feel dislike
2. *dejected* by a poor mark	(b) something thought about, talked about, or studied
3. *object* to the plan	(c) turned down; thrown back
4. *eject* a noisy boy	(d) made sad
5. *subject* of a speech	(e) throw out

A Little Harder: Fill in the blanks. Find the correct *ject* word from the list above for each of the following sentences and write it in your notebook.

1. "I _____ to the low mark you gave me," Don said to his teacher.
2. The police will _____ them from the game because they were fighting.
3. What was the _____ of your composition?
4. Olga was _____ when her boy friend left for the army.

170

5. Tony was ⎯⎯⎯⎯⎯ when he went for that job, because he hadn't finished high school.

EXPRESSING YOURSELF

1. What insect or animal do you dislike the most? Why?

2. Look up the story of yellow fever in an encyclopedia or some other reference book. Then tell the class how scientists finally found a cure for it. (You might want to read the play *Yellow Jack* by Sidney Howard, which tells the story in a most interesting way.)

3. Do mosquitoes like you? Write a paragraph telling about your run-ins with mosquitoes.

4. If you were a mosquito, which kind of person would you like to bite? Why?

24. BALDY THE BALANCING CLOWN

WHAT'S THE BEST TRICK YOU EVER SAW SOMEBODY DO?

HAVE YOU EVER SEEN TRICKS LIKE THE ONES THAT BALDY THE BALANCING CLOWN DOES?

WEST ISLIP, N.Y., March 24 — The army *sergeant* lifted the heavy typewriter and walked around with it balanced on his chin.

172

He carried the typewriter on his chin, Sergeant Marvin Fox said, because he was afraid it might *squash* his nose.

Sergeant Fox is better known to children all over the world as "Baldy the Balancing Clown." Among other things, he can balance seven chairs on his chin.

One of Baldy's most *exciting* tricks is to balance twenty butcher knives on a *disk spinning* on top of a seven-foot pole while he plays a tune on the organ.

Once, while performing in Berlin, Germany, he missed. Suddenly, the butcher knives came *crashing* down into his leg and he was rushed to the hospital. "It is a dangerous trick," Baldy said, *shrugging*, "but that's part of the business."

How did Sergeant Fox become Baldy the Balancing Clown? It began when he was growing up in an *orphanage* in New York City. He often had to help out in the kitchen, and to make time go faster, he began balancing pots and pans on his chin. Soon he went to brooms, mops, pails, plates, knives and eggs. His chin became rock-hard.

At fifteen, he ran away and joined a circus. At sixteen, he faked his age and *joined* the army. It was with the army in Germany that he got his first taste of *fame*. He had his own television show. He also did an act he called "Baldy the Human Seal." In it, he balanced a seventeen-foot pole topped by a pair of chairs — while swimming in a pool!

— NEWSDAY (Long Island, N.Y.)

173

CHECK YOUR UNDERSTANDING

1. Another title that would best explain the main idea of this story is:
   (a) An Army Sergeant
   (b) Growing up in an Orphanage
   (c) An Amazing Clown
   (d) Life in Germany
2. Marvin Fox grew up in
   (a) an orphanage.
   (b) Germany.
   (c) the army.
   (d) a circus.
3. Sergeant Fox began balancing things on his chin to
   (a) make his chin rock-hard.
   (b) help out in the kitchen.
   (c) get into show business.
   (d) make time go faster in the kitchen.
4. At sixteen, Sergeant Fox
   (a) ran away and joined a circus.
   (b) became a sergeant in the army.
   (c) had his own television show.
   (d) joined the army by faking his age.
5. In the trick in which Baldy plays a tune on the organ, he balances
   (a) a seventeen-foot pole topped by a pair of chairs.
   (b) twenty butcher knives.
   (c) seven chairs.
   (d) a typewriter.

REACHING OUT

1. One thing this story does *not* say Baldy balanced on his chin was
   (a) a swimming pool.
   (b) a typewriter.
   (c) a seventeen-foot pole.
   (d) twenty butcher knives.
2. We can guess from this story that Marvin Fox has entertained
   (a) only in the United States.
   (b) only in Germany.
   (c) only in the United States and Germany.
   (d) in many countries of the world.

FIRST THINGS FIRST

Arrange these things in the order in which Marvin Fox did them.

1. He joined the army.
2. He had his own television show.
3. He first learned to balance pots and pans on his chin.
4. He joined a circus.
5. He was put into an orphanage.
6. He learned to balance brooms and mops on his chin.

175

IMPROVING YOUR VOCABULARY

In the first column below and on the next page are the ten words in italics from the story. Pick out the best "story" meaning of each of these words.

1. army *sergeant* (a) army officer above rank of corporal; (b) the lowest rank in the army; (c) army rank just below captain

2. *squash* his nose (a) crush; (b) hit; (c) tickle

3. *exciting* trick (a) thrilling; (b) easy; (c) difficult

4. knives on a *disk* (a) cup; (b) something heavy and square; (c) something flat, thin and round

5. *spinning* on a pole (a) balanced; (b) turning around quickly; (c) jumping up and down

6. *crashing* down (a) shouting; (b) hitting with force; (c) falling softly and easily

7. said *shrugging* (a) raising the shoulders; (b) lying; (c) giving an opinion

8. grew up in an *orphanage* (a) bad part of a city; (b) home for children without parents; (c) a special school

9. *joined* the army (a) ran away from; (b)

tried to get into; (c) became a member of

10. taste of *fame*   (a) good food and drink; (b) happiness; (c) being very well-known

---

WORD BUILDING

The word *performing* in the story above means *acting, playing, singing or doing tricks in public.* The second part of the word, *forming,* comes from a French word which means *carrying out,* or *completing.* The prefix *per* means *through. Performing,* then, has the sense of *carrying something through to the end.*

The prefix *per* usually means *through,* although sometimes it may mean *very.*

Example: *perspire* means *to breathe through,* therefore, *to sweat.*

To Do: Match the meaning in column B to the proper *per* word in column A.

A	**B**
1. *perfect* your work	(a) let; allow
2. *permanent* peace	(b) win over to do or to believe
3. *permit* to enter	(c) carry through; complete
4. *persuade* the people	(d) stick to it; stay through
5. *persist* in trying	(e) lasting; remaining through the years

A Little Harder: Fill in the blanks. Find the correct "per" word from the list above for each of the following sentences and write it in your notebook.

1. "I cannot _____ you to come in here without a pass," the man at the door said.
2. The man from Tennessee said that he hoped to make New York City his _____ home.
3. Why do you _____ in doing things that will only cause you trouble?
4. As he continued speaking, he began to _____ his listeners that he was right.
5. The artist works for years on his paintings in order to _____ them.

EXPRESSING YOURSELF

1. Marvin Fox learned his tricks to keep from being bored while working in the orphanage kitchen. Tell about some of the ways you pass the time when you don't have very much to do.
2. Do you think it was wrong of Baldy to fake his age in order to join the army? Why?
3. Describe your favorite entertainer.
4. Sergeant Fox was a soldier and a clown. Write a paragraph telling what work you plan to do when you finish school.

25. NEWARK'S NEGRO POLICE CAPTAIN

THE NEGRO IN AMERICA HAS HAD DOORS TO ADVANCEMENT CLOSED AGAINST HIM. HAS THERE BEEN A CHANGE FOR THE BETTER IN RECENT YEARS?

HOW MIGHT CAPTAIN EDWARD WILLIAMS REPLY TO THAT QUESTION?

NEWARK, N.J., Mar. 2 — Captain Edward Williams today became the first Negro to take *command* of Newark's Central Ward. That area is an almost all-Negro section of the city.

Just eight months ago, in five days of *rioting* in Newark, 26 persons were killed and more than 1,000 injured. The *appointment* of a Negro captain is an important step in bringing better understanding and *cooperation* between Central Ward and its police force.

Captain Williams told reporters how it felt to be a Negro in Newark in the nineteen-thirties. He remembered going to a city swimming pool with other Negro youths on a hot summer day. They were turned away and told: "Your day is Friday." He *recollected* that he and his friends could use only the balcony in *certain* movie theaters.

He was brought up near the police station, and the building filled him with *dread*. "We used to lower our voices when we passed it. And we all believed they had a whipping machine for kids in the basement, a machine that gave kids a spanking."

The captain laughed and said that as soon as he has a *spare* moment he is going down to the basement. He wants to investigate for himself just what is there. "If I find a spanking machine, I'll throw it out."

Captain Williams was born in Tampa, Florida, but his parents moved to Newark when he was two years old. He became a policeman because he wanted the *"security"* of the job. While a sergeant, he won a *scholarship* to Seton Hall University. He was graduated in 1960, an expert in police science.

— NEW YORK TIMES

CHECK YOUR UNDERSTANDING

1. Another title that would best explain the main idea of this story is:
   (a) Newark's Central Ward
   (b) Growing Up in Newark
   (c) Job Security
   (d) Negro Police Officer Takes Charge
2. Edward Williams was accepted at Seton Hall University because he was
   (a) poor.
   (b) lucky.
   (c) intelligent.
   (d) a high school graduate.
3. The appointment of Captain Williams to Newark's Central Ward is important because
   (a) he will help in bringing better understanding between the people and the police force.
   (b) he grew up in Newark.
   (c) the police station in the Central Ward must be rebuilt.
   (d) the job has security.
4. When Captain Williams and his friends were young
   (a) policemen treated them to free movies.
   (b) they thought that the police station had a spanking machine.
   (c) they were arrested.
   (d) they made noise every time they passed the police station.
5. Captain Williams became a policeman because he wanted
   (a) to become a captain.

(b) to go to college.

(c) job security.

(d) to check on the spanking machine.

REACHING OUT

1. In the nineteen-thirties, Captain Williams and his friends could not
   (a) go swimming six days of the week.
   (b) go swimming on Fridays.
   (c) sit in the balcony of a movie theater.
   (d) pass a police station.
2. When Captain Williams spoke of the spanking machine in the basement of the police station, his mood was most likely
   (a) angry.
   (b) good-humored.
   (c) upset.
   (d) serious.

PUTTING THE PIECES TOGETHER

Below is a title for each of the six paragraphs in the story. Put these titles in the order in which the paragraphs appeared in the story. The first one is done for you.

1. Newark Riots
2. Why Captain Williams Became a Policeman
3. Captain Williams Chosen for Central Ward— Paragraph 1
4. Living in Newark in the 1930's

5. A Basement Investigation
6. Fear of the Police Station

IMPROVING YOUR VOCABULARY

In the first column below are the ten words in italics from the story. Pick out the best "story" meaning of each of these words.

1. to take *command* — (a) to take out; (b) to take charge; (c) to order
2. *rioting* in Newark — (a) behaving wildly; (b) spilling; (c) building
3. *appointment* of a new captain — (a) meeting; (b) charging; (c) naming to a job
4. better *cooperation* — (a) working together; (b) charging; (c) talking
5. *recollected* the past — (a) forgot; (b) remembered; (c) wrote about
6. *certain* movie theaters — (a) perfect; (b) all; (c) some
7. filled with *dread* — (a) great fear; (b) dead people; (c) color
8. a *spare* moment — (a) extra; (b) busy; (c) little
9. *security* of the job — (a) danger; (b) loss; (c) safety
10. *scholarship* to college — (a) student; (b) high marks; (c) money to help pay for an education

WORD BUILDING

The word *scholarship* means a reward (usually money) given to students to help them continue with their studies. It is given when a student has done excellent work in the past.

Explanation: The stem *scholar* means a student who has gained much knowledge

The suffix *ship* means *the condition of being* or *the skill of*.

When you put the two meanings together, *scholarship* means the skill of being a scholar. Therefore, when a student has studied a great deal and passed his courses with high marks, he reveals his *scholarship* (his skill as a student). For this success, he sometimes is rewarded with a *scholarship* (money to help him continue his studies).

The suffix *ship* almost always means *the condition of being,* or *the skill of*.

To Do: Write the meaning of each of the underlined *ship* words in your notebook. The first one is done for you.

1. the *friendship* of Damon and Pythias — being a *friend*
2. *membership* in a club — being a _____
3. the power of the *governorship* — being a _____
4. a *partnership* in the business — being a _____
5. the lawyer received a *judgeship* — being a _____

EXPRESSING YOURSELF

1. "How does it feel to be the first Negro captain of Newark's Central Ward?" asked the reporter. What do you think Captain Williams would answer?
2. When he was young, Captain Williams was treated unfairly in a swimming pool because of prejudice. Tell about an instance when you or someone you know has experienced prejudice.
3. Write a paragraph telling about some member of a minority group who had to struggle to become successful.
4. It sometimes helps in applying for scholarships and jobs to know that a student has been active in after-school or community affairs. What kind of activities would you suggest? Why?

Mosquitoes

Some people attract twice as
many mosquitoes as others do.
How come?

REVIEW OF LESSONS 21-25

IMPROVING YOUR VOCABULARY

Choose the correct meaning of each of the words below. (The number in parentheses after each word tells you the story the word was first tested in.)

1. accept (22)   (a) leave; (b) take willingly; (c) ask

2. adjoining (21)   (a) above; (b) across; (c) next to

3. alarm (21)   (a) fill with fear suddenly; (b) catch; (c) hurt deeply

4. appointment (25)   (a) naming to a job; (b) line; (c) charging

186

5. appreciation (22) (a) sorrow; (b) happiness; (c) thankfulness

6. arrived (22) (a) went by; (b) came to a certain point; (c) went away

7. attract (23) (a) push; (b) bite; (c) draw to oneself

8. avoid (23) (a) keep away from; (b) invite; (c) to empty

9. certain (25) (a) all; (b) some; (c) none

10. citizenship (22) (a) being a member of a country; (b) boat of travelers; (c) prize

11. command (25) (a) to calm; (b) to take charge; (c) to beat

12. cooperation (25) (a) talking; (b) working together; (c) getting well

13. crashing (24) (a) yelling; (b) hitting with force; (c) falling softly

14. curling (21) (a) calling out; (b) jumping; (c) rising in rings

15. disease (23) (a) illness; (b) death; (c) accident

16. disobeys (21) (a) gives orders; (b) listens quietly; (c) does not do what one is told

17. disk (24) (a) cup; (b) place to work; (c) something flat, thin and round

18. dread (25)   (a) great fear; (b) bread; (c) dry

19. excellent (21)   (a) very good; (b) unwanted; (c) passing

20. exciting (24)   (a) unsafe; (b) uninteresting; (c) thrilling

21. experts (23)   (a) people who know a lot about some special thing; (b) people who sell; (c) people who travel

22. faith (22)   (a) worry; (b) trust; (c) happiness

23. fame (24)   (a) good food; (b) not wild; (c) being very well known

24. female (23)   (a) the man with a family; (b) the sex that brings forth young; (c) another kind

25. frequently (23)   (a) often; (b) less and less; (c) strange

26. inject (23)   (a) put back; (b) force into; (c) throw out

27. immigrant (22)   (a) hard worker; (b) kind person; (c) person who comes from one country to another to live

28. joined (24)   (a) tried to get into; (b) became a member of; (c) went away

29. obedient (21)

(a) good at household duties; (b) sick in bed; (c) doing what one is told

30. opportunity (22)

(a) good plan; (b) good tune; (c) good chance

31. orphanage (24)

(a) home for children without parents; (b) hospital; (c) home for old people

32. pounded (21)

(a) hit hard again and again; (b) tap gently; (c) put on a scale to weigh.

33. protect (22)

(a) keep from harm; (b) hurt; (c) give back

34. proud (22)

(a) rich; (b) wise; (c) thinking well of oneself

35. recollected (25)

(a) added; (b) put away; (c) remembered

36. repellent (23)

(a) sweet smell; (b) something used to keep insects away; (c) rain

37. replied (21)

(a) answered; (b) did twice; (c) told the facts

38. responsible (21)

(a) able to be trusted; (b) old; (c) young

39. rioting (25)

(a) wasting; (b) building; (c) behaving wildly

40. saliva (23)

(a) salt; (b) liquid in the mouth; (c) illness

41. scholarship (25)   (a) money given to help pay for an education; (b) job; (c) college

42. security (25)   (a) safety; (b) danger; (c) loss

43. sergeant (24)   (a) army truck; (b) army rank just above captain; (c) army officer above the rank of corporal

44. shrugging (24)   (a) holding tightly; (b) raising the shoulders; (c) fighting

45. spare (25)   (a) fat; (b) extra; (c) bowling ball

46. spinning (24)   (a) tying down; (b) knitting; (c) turning around quickly

47. squash (24)   (a) crush; (b) run from; (c) carry

48. swollen (23)   (a) smaller than usual; (b) great; (c) larger than usual

49. tense (21)   (a) more than ten; (b) nervous; (c) thick

50. wealthy (22)   (a) poor; (b) rich; (c) happy

WORD BUILDING

Match the meaning in column B to the proper word-building part in column A.

	A			**B**
1. *ject* (23)			(a)	in front of; before; forward
2. *ship* (25)			(b)	throw
3. *ad* (21)			(c)	through; very
4. *per* (24)			(d)	to; toward
5. *pro* (22)			(e)	the condition of being; the skill of

WORD BUILDING

Pick out the proper meaning for each word in the first column.

1. address (21)

(a) speak to; (b) take off clothing; (c) be neat

2. adhesive (21)

(a) something that sticks to things; (b) water; (c) crayon

3. adjust (21)

(a) fit to; (b) put off; (c) run away

4. advance (21)

(a) go toward; (b) leave from; (c) leave before

5. advertise (21)

(a) call people's attention to; (b) turn in; (c) sell

6. dejected (23)

(a) made dirty; (b) made sad; (c) made happy

7. eject (23)

(a) build up; (b) throw out; (c) pull down

8. to object (23)

(a) to be against; (b) to be for; (c) to fail

191

9. to perfect (24)   (a) to escape; (b) to complete; (c) to follow

10. permanent (24)   (a) beauty parlor; (b) passing; (c) lasting

11. to permit (24)   (a) to buy; (b) to sell; (c) to let or allow

12. persist (24)   (a) refuse to stop; (b) give up; (c) make agree

13. persuade (24)   (a) win over; (b) get tired; (c) shine

14. proceed (22)   (a) go before; (b) go back; (c) go forward

15. projector (22)   (a) flashlight; (b) machine that throws pictures forward on a screen; (c) large building

16. promotion (22)   (a) moving back in rank; (b) moving forward in rank; (c) standing still

17. propel (22)   (a) drive forward; (b) correct; (c) let fall

18. propose (22)   (a) order; (b) support; (c) suggest

19. rejected (23)   (a) was angry; (b) was against; (c) turned down

20. subject (23)   (a) something for; (b) something against; (c) something thought or talked about

26. HOW DOES A WITCH DOCTOR WORK?

CAN A WITCH DOCTOR REALLY CURE PEOPLE?

MILLIONS OF PEOPLE ARE SURE THAT HE CAN!

Malaysia is a country in Asia that has seven million people. In many ways, Malaysia is modern, but people still visit their bomoh. The bomoh

(BO-MO), or witch doctor, still plays an *important* role in the life of the country.

Last week, the king of Malaysia went to a state in the northern part of the country. A bomoh was called upon to make sure that it didn't rain for three days. It didn't.

The bomoh does more than stop the rain. People go to him for advice on anything and everything. He will tell them the best time to plant crops, when to go fishing and the "right time" to get married.

He is best known, however, for his power to *cure* the sick. How does he do this? Let us *suppose* someone who has a burning *fever* is taken to a bomoh. After examining his patient, the bomoh will sit cross-legged on a special rug with a glass of water before him. Into the water he drops, one by one, the petals of a rose. Then he *crushes* the center of the flower and drops that among the petals. He then *stirs* the *mixture*.

If the petals fall to the bottom of the glass there is no hope. If they remain on top, he asks for another glass of water. Using the "right" *method,* he takes a mouthful of water from the second glass and sprays it over the patient.

It is hard to understand why this often brings down the fever. Most probably, it is faith in the bomoh that does it. After all, *emotional* upset can cause illness just as easily as germs can. Belief by the people in the *power* of the witch doctor to cure might help to drive away emotional upset and so cure the illness.

At any rate, the bomoh is still a very busy man.

— SAN FRANCISCO CHRONICLE

CHECK YOUR UNDERSTANDING

1. Another title that would best explain the main idea of this story is:
   (a) The King and the Bomoh
   (b) The Bomoh and the Weather
   (c) Curing the Sick
   (d) The Bomoh's Work

2. The bomoh is a very important person in Malaysia because
   (a) there are seven million people there.
   (b) he gives secret advice to the king.
   (c) people seek his advice on everything.
   (d) he knows the secrets of modern medicine.

3. If you were to visit the bomoh, the first thing he would probably do is
   (a) sit cross-legged on a rug.
   (b) examine you.
   (c) say a prayer.
   (d) drink some water with flower petals in it.

4. In this story, one of the ways the bomoh finds out if he can cure a patient is by
   (a) asking when he plans to get married.
   (b) checking to see if petals fall to the bottom of a glass of water.
   (c) checking the weather conditions.
   (d) fishing.

5. When the bomoh sees the petals fall to the bottom of the glass, he knows that
   (a) it is the right time for a person to marry.
   (b) it will rain.
   (c) he cannot cure his patient.
   (d) it is the right time to plant crops.

REACHING OUT

1. One thing the bomoh did not give advice on in this story is
   (a) the "right time" to get married.
   (b) the best time to plant crops.
   (c) the best time to build a house.
   (d) the best time to go fishing.
2. A modern doctor would most likely explain the success of the witch doctor by saying that
   (a) he uses the right medicine.
   (b) he chooses only patients that he can cure.
   (c) he has special powers that doctors do not have.
   (d) the people he cures believe in him and are usually sick from emotional upset.
3. When the king went to the northern part of Malaysia and it didn't rain, this proved
   (a) that the bomoh really could make rain.
   (b) that the bomoh really couldn't make rain.
   (c) nothing.
   (d) that the bomoh can make anything he wants happen.

PUTTING THE PIECES TOGETHER

Below is a title for each of the seven paragraphs in the story. Put these titles in the order in which the paragraphs appeared in the story. The first one is done for you.

1. The Bomoh and the Prayer Rug
2. About Malaysia—Paragraph 1
3. Why the Bomoh's Method Works

4. The King's Trip
5. The Type of Advice That the Bomoh Gives
6. The Bomoh Decides If the Sick Person Will Live or Die
7. The Bomoh Is Busy

IMPROVING YOUR VOCABULARY

In the first column below and on the next page are the ten words in italics from the story. Pick out the best "story" meaning of each of these words.

1. *important* job — (a) dangerous; (b) part-time; (c) valuable or worth notice

2. *cure* the sick — (a) make well; (b) talk nicely; (c) hurt

3. let's *suppose* it is summer — (a) go; (b) hope; (c) imagine

4. a burning *fever* — (a) low body temperature; (b) thermometer; (c) high body temperature

5. *crushes* the flower — (a) wets completely; (b) breaks into small pieces; (c) does quickly

6. *stirs* the ice cream soda — (a) mixes; (b) lifts high; (c) drinks quickly

7. paint *mixture* — (a) that which has been eaten; (b) that which has been prepared by putting different things together; (c) that which has been folded

197

8. the right *method*   (a) way of singing; (b) way of doing something; (c) tool

9. an *emotional* person   (a) quiet; (b) sick; (c) having strong feelings

10. *power* of the witch doctor   (a) electricity; (b) weakness; (c) might

---

WORD BUILDING

The word *mixture* in the story means something that has been mixed, or the result of mixing things together. The suffix *ure* means either *the result of an act* or *the act of*.

To Do: In your notebook, write the meaning of each of these words ending in *ure,* which means here *result of.* Use the "ing" form of the word shown for you in the parentheses. The first one is done for you.

1. signature (signing)—the result of signing

2. seizure (seizing)

3. pressure (pressing)

4. pleasure (pleasing)

5. exposure (exposing)

A Little Harder: Match the meaning in column B to the proper *ure* word in column A.

A	B
1. *fracture* an arm	(a) free time
2. *capture* an enemy	(b) slight wetness
3. *leisure* hours	(c) break
4. *moisture* in the air	(d) catch
5. a wall *fixture*	(e) thing put in place to stay

198

EXPRESSING YOURSELF

1. Tell of some "folk remedies" or cures that people still use. Do they work? If so, why?
2. If you were a doctor in Malaysia, how would you prove to your patients that your methods would be better for them than those of a witch doctor?
3. Many people are "superstitious." They believe in magic or chance and are afraid of natural things. Are you nervous around black cats, or during a full moon or when you break a mirror? Do you know anyone who is superstitious?
4. Write a paragraph telling why you would, or would not, like to be a doctor.

27. RESCUE IN A BURNING BUILDING

DID YOU EVER HAVE TO MAKE A QUICK DECISION?

WHAT WOULD YOU HAVE DONE IF YOU WERE ONE OF THESE FIREMEN?

NEW YORK, June 17 — A fireman rescued a 76-year-old woman from a burning apartment building yesterday by tossing her off a fire escape. The woman, Mrs. Mary Rogers, landed safely in the arms of another fireman waiting on the roof of an adjoining building.

Fireman Edward Lane had *risked* his life to reach the woman, who was trapped in her smoke-filled top-floor apartment in the five-story building. The fire was *blazing* out of control as Lane carried the almost *unconscious* woman onto a fire escape.

As flames *threatened* them, Lane tried without *success* to first climb to the roof and then to go below the *height* of the flames. He could not do so while carrying the dead weight of the helpless 115-pound woman.

Then he saw another fireman, Mike Mays, *motioning* to him with his arms held out. Mays was on the roof of the next building, which was level with the fire escape. A space of only four feet

separated the two buildings, but there was a fifty-foot drop to the ground. Lane tried to pass Mrs. Rogers over to Mays, but the *gap* was too wide.

Then the two men decided that the only chance to save the woman was to try something very dangerous. Lane reached back and threw Mrs. Rogers across the space between the buildings. For a moment the woman was not *supported* above the ground. Then Mays caught her by the neck and shoulders, and pulled her safely onto the roof. Mrs. Rogers was uninjured.

Lane then climbed to the roof of the burning building, went down another fire escape and back to fighting the fire.

— NEWSDAY (Long Island, N.Y.)

CHECK YOUR UNDERSTANDING

1. Another title that would best explain the main idea of this story is:
   (a) Fire Rescue
   (b) Flying Between Buildings
   (c) Two Firemen
   (d) An Unconscious Old Lady
2. After Edward Lane saved Mrs. Rogers, he
   (a) helped carry her downstairs.
   (b) went back to fight the fire.
   (c) stopped to rest.
   (d) helped her come back to life.
3. Probably, the 76-year-old woman was unconscious because

(a) she tripped and fell.

(b) she became dizzy from yelling.

(c) the fireman could carry her easily.

(d) she breathed in too much smoke.

4. Lane decided to toss Mrs. Rogers over to the next building because

(a) he was strong.

(b) Mrs. Rogers told him to.

(c) he was getting dizzy.

(d) it was the only way to get her to safety.

5. Lane could not pass Mrs. Rogers to Mays because

(a) she was too heavy.

(b) the space between the buildings was too wide.

(c) Mrs. Rogers kept slipping from his hands.

(d) the flames from the fire were too close.

REACHING OUT

1. One thing Edward Lane did *not* do was

(a) risk his own life.

(b) take a chance with the life of Mrs. Rogers.

(c) climb to the roof of the burning building.

(d) get Mike Mays to help rescue Mrs. Rogers.

2. The one of the following that did *not* happen in the story was that

(a) Lane threw Mrs. Rogers to Mays.

(b) the fire was out of control in Mrs. Rogers' apartment.

(c) a fire escape caved in.

(d) Mrs. Rogers was unconscious.

FIRST THINGS FIRST

Arrange these events in the order in which they happened.

1. Edward Lane dragged Mrs. Rogers outside onto a fire escape.
2. Mays motioned to Lane on the roof.
3. Lane tried to climb to the roof.
4. Mrs. Rogers was unconscious in her smoke-filled apartment.
5. Lane threw Mrs. Rogers to Mays.
6. A fire began to blaze out of control in a five-story building.

GETTING THE PICTURE

Pick out the words in the second column that will finish the pictures started in the first column. The correct answer for the first one is (c) "A fire . . . was blazing out of control."

A	B
1. A fire	(a) caught the woman by the neck and shoulders.
2. Mike Mays	
3. Mrs. Rogers	(b) was five stories high.
4. The building	(c) was blazing out of control.
5. Edward Lane	
	(d) reached back and threw Mrs. Rogers from one building to another.
	(e) was unconscious in a smoke-filled apartment.

IMPROVING YOUR VOCABULARY

In the first column below are the ten words in italics from the story. Pick out the best "story" meaning of each of these words.

1. *risked* his life — (a) gave; (b) took a dangerous chance with; (c) saved

2. *blazing* out of control — (a) flaming; (b) flying; (c) jumping

3. the woman was *unconscious* — (a) unable to sleep; (b) unable to feel or be aware; (c) unable to talk

4. the flames *threatened* — (a) became dangerous; (b) died out; (c) were hot

5. without *success* — (a) good results; (b) failing; (c) leadership

6. the *height* of the building — (a) how long something is; (b) how wide something is; (c) how tall something is

7. *motioning* with his arms — (a) carrying; (b) pushing; (c) showing what he meant

8. *separated* by a few feet — (a) joined or together; (b) touching; (c) drawn apart or divided

9. a wide *gap* — (a) angle; (b) space; (c) hat

10. *supported* with steel — (a) tied up; (b) made of; (c) held up

WORD BUILDING

The word *motioning* in the story means moving a part of your body to tell something to someone. Most people motion with their hands, but they sometimes use other parts of the body. For instance, when you want to tell someone to kick a tin can, you can motion with your leg better than with your hands.

The stem *mot* means to move. It is helpful to remember it with another stem, *mov*, which also means to move. When you see *mov* or *mot* in a word, you will know that the word deals with movement of some kind.

To Do: Match the meaning in column B to the proper *mov* or *mot* word in column A.

A	B
1. motor	(a) pictures that move quickly
2. motive	(b) able to be moved
3. promote	(c) to move ahead
4. movies	(d) an engine that makes a machine go
5. movable	(e) the thought or feeling that makes someone do something

A Little Harder: Add one of these endings to the stem *mov* to make a word for each of the meanings listed below. Write the word in your notebook. The first one is done for you.

MOV
- + er — a person who
- + ed — past tense of move
- + able — able to
- + ment — act of

1. A person who moves things is a ___mover___.
2. Something you are able to move is _____.
3. The act of moving is called _____.
4. When I was asked to move the desk yesterday, I _____ it.

EXPRESSING YOURSELF

1. Write about the quickest decision that you ever made. What was the problem and what last-minute choices ran through your mind before you took action?
2. A fireman receives special training in fighting and preventing fires. Find out about his job by getting information from your career adviser or library in school or by asking members of your local fire department.
3. Tell about some person you know or read about who was brave in the face of danger.
4. In the city, a fire in an apartment building can threaten a great many lives. During such a fire, how can each person's actions cut down on or increase the danger?

28. THE UNDER-STANDING WIDOW

WOULD YOU REALLY RISK YOUR LIFE TO SAVE SOMEONE ELSE?

FIND OUT WHAT MR. AND MRS. DAVID TERRY DID WHEN FACED WITH THIS QUESTION.

Mrs. Barbara Terry could never understand why her husband gave up his life to save others. Her husband, Sergeant David Terry, was killed in Vietnam when he threw himself upon a live *grenade* to save his *patrol*.

Yesterday Mrs. Terry did understand.

"It's human *instinct*," said the 27-year-old widow. She had just *plunged* into Aurora Lake to save a woman and five boys when their car ran into the water.

"I didn't think of myself," she said. "I heard those kids scream and that was all I needed."

Mrs. Terry was fishing at the lake Wednesday afternoon with her two children when the accident occurred. A car driven by Mrs. Louis Curtis *skidded* off the *freshly* oiled road and plunged into the lake. With Mrs. Curtis were her two boys and a neighbor's three sons.

Mrs. Terry heard the *shrieks* of the children and turned to see the car *submerge*. She swam to the car and helped the boys and Mrs. Curtis through the open windows to safety on the automobile roof. Then, one by one, she swam with them to shore.

It was the first time Mrs. Terry had been to the lake since her husband had taken the family there before he went overseas.

Sergeant Terry was killed, but the other members of his patrol *survived*.

— SAN FRANCISCO CHRONICLE

CHECK YOUR UNDERSTANDING

1. Another title that would best explain the main idea of this story is:
   (a) Soldier Dies to Save Others
   (b) Auto Plunges into Lake

(c) Heroes from the Same Family

(d) Fishing in Aurora Lake

2. Mrs. Terry explained that she dived into the lake because
   (a) she thought of her husband.
   (b) she heard the children's screams.
   (c) she wanted to save her children.
   (d) she wanted to die.

3. Sergeant David Terry
   (a) threw himself on a grenade at Aurora Lake.
   (b) saved his men from a sinking car.
   (c) was fishing at Aurora Lake.
   (d) saved the lives of his men.

4. Mrs. Curtis' car plunged into the lake because
   (a) she lost control of the car.
   (b) she heard the screams of Mrs. Terry's children.
   (c) the car slid on an oiled road.
   (d) she was thinking of her husband.

5. Mrs. Terry saved the lives of
   (a) one adult and five children.
   (b) two adults and four children.
   (c) three children.
   (d) six children.

REACHING OUT

1. Mrs. Terry did *not*
   (a) swim to the automobile that sank.
   (b) throw herself on a grenade.
   (c) see the car sink.
   (d) find out why her husband gave up his life.

2. From her experience, Mrs. Terry learned
- (a) that it doesn't pay to be a hero.
- (b) that people should never drive automobiles.
- (c) what made her husband throw himself on a grenade.
- (d) why her children became scared.

FIRST THINGS FIRST

Arrange these events in the order in which they happened.

1. A car plunged into the lake.
2. One by one, Mrs. Terry swam to shore with each member of the family.
3. Mrs. Terry heard the screams of the children.
4. David Terry threw himself on a hand grenade.
5. Mrs. Terry was fishing with her children on Aurora Lake.
6. Mrs. Terry dived into the lake.
7. Mrs. Terry helped the Curtis family through the open windows of the car.

SIGHTS AND SOUNDS

When you read, you not only form "pictures" in your imagination of things that happen in a story. Sometimes you can even imagine sounds. Pick out the words in the second column that will finish the picture or sound started in the first column.

A	**B**
1. Sergeant David Terry	(a) heard the shrieks of the children in the Curtis' car.
2. Mrs. Louis Curtis' car	
3. Mrs. Terry	(b) threw himself upon a live hand grenade.
4. Mrs. Curtis' boys	
5. Mrs. Terry's children	(c) came to safety through the open car window.
	(d) were fishing at Aurora Lake.
	(e) skidded on a freshly oiled road and submerged.

IMPROVING YOUR VOCABULARY

In the first column below and on the next page are the ten words in italics from the story. Pick out the best "story" meaning of each of these words.

1. a *grenade* blew up	(a) drink; (b) small bomb; (c) fruit
2. save his *patrol*	(a) group of soldiers; (b) fuel; (c) brother
3. *instinct* to live	(a) moment; (b) smell; (c) feeling to act
4. a *widow*	(a) space for light; (b) woman whose husband is dead; (c) bug
5. *plunged* into the lake	(a) ran; (b) dived; (c) swam

6. *skidded* off the highway	(a) flew; (b) crashed; (c) slid sideways
7. *freshly* painted	(a) angrily; (b) newly; (c) nicely
8. *shrieks* of the children	(a) bedcovers; (b) Arab people; (c) sharp loud sounds
9. see the car *submerge*	(a) sink; (b) float on water; (c) make bubbles
10. *survived* the accident	(a) passed out food; (b) died; (c) stayed alive

---

WORD BUILDING

"Mrs. Terry . . . turned to see the car submerge."

From the way *submerge* is used in this sentence you know that the word means *to put under water* or *to sink.* Another clue to the meaning of the word is the prefix *sub,* which means *under.*

To Do: Add *sub* to each of these words to form a new word and write the new word in your notebook. The first one is done for you.

1. marine   submarine
2. way   _____
3. title   _____
4. soil   _____
5. mit   _____

Find the meaning of each of the words you just wrote from the list of meanings on the next page. Copy it in your notebook.

1. a second title that goes under a main title
2. a boat that can go under water
3. the layer of earth that is right under the top of the soil
4. an electric train that runs under street level
5. surrender to people who have power or authority

A Little Harder: Match the meaning in column B to the proper *sub* word in column A.

A	**B**
1. a *substance* in soap	(a) to separate into smaller parts
2. to *subdue* the enemy	
3. to *subdivide* the land	(b) to defeat
4. to *substitute* for a player	(c) to take the place of another
5. *substandard* machine	(d) not as good as expected
	(e) the stuff from which something is made

EXPRESSING YOURSELF

1. Imagine that Sergeant David Terry had saved your life when he fell on the grenade. In a paragraph, tell how you would feel about what he did.
2. Decorations and medals are usually given to people who do brave deeds. Most medals are given to men and women who serve in the armed forces of their country. However, medals are also given to civilians (people or citizens of

a country). To whom would you award a medal for one of the following good deeds, and why?
(a) heroism in the face of danger
(b) service to one's school or community
(c) achievement in a special field
3. Do you think someone has to be brave in everyday life? If so, what kind of bravery is needed? Would it be different from that shown by Mr. and Mrs. Terry? Explain your answer.

29. TRAFFIC TOREADOR

HOW WELL DO YOU KNOW POLICEMEN?

WOULD YOU LIKE PATROLMAN CHARLES J. EVERETT IF YOU WERE TO MEET HIM?

You've heard about the singing traffic cop who cheers motorists with his gay tunes. But how about a dancing cop? The town of Alliance, Ohio, has one: Patrolman Charlie J. Everett, a six-foot-two, 210-pound dance act in traffic.

One motorist said that when Everett directs traffic, he looks like a *fearless, graceful* toreador (or bullfighter). The unusual skill and *enthusiasm* that brings Everett to his job of keeping traffic *flowing* have not escaped notice. He has won the attention and praise of the entire *community*.

When Everett takes over an *intersection,* he runs it with "body English"—smooth arm and hand movements, and sharp whistle blasts. His white gloves spin zigzag *patterns* in the air as he starts moving traffic. His arms sweep around and stop suddenly as he points with his index finger at cars to halt. His body twists, dips and bends, and to passing motorists, he looks as if he were dancing.

Everett is more *practical* than a toreador, whose major job is to entertain. He has fun directing traffic, but he takes his job seriously.

"I don't mind stopping for him," says Steve Sigmund, a driver who has to pilot a *huge,* steel-loaded truck through town. "I know he'll get me started in time to make the light. He knows what it means to keep a big *rig* moving. He's not working against me."

Charles Everett joined the police force after quitting a job in a metal-works factory. One day a road-building company asked for an off-duty policeman to direct traffic around paving crews. Everett offered to help and never forgot the day.

"It must have been over 100 degrees," Everett said of his first traffic job. "The sun was shining off the road, and the car smells added to the heat. Traffic kept getting thicker and thicker. Another patrolman and I stood back to back for forty-five minutes trying to control traffic. Under the broiling sun, the tar was so hot it became soft, and the crews were using water to cool it. We got traffic moving and cleared up the jam. I wanted to come back someday and run the intersection by myself."

— EBONY

CHECK YOUR UNDERSTANDING

1. Another title that would best explain the main idea of this story is:
   (a) How to Direct Traffic
   (b) Building Roads
   (c) Bullfighting
   (d) A Talented Traffic Cop
2. Charles Everett is a very unusual traffic cop because
   (a) people stop to talk to him.
   (b) he has long arms.
   (c) he directs the intersection with exciting movements.
   (d) truck drivers trust him.
3. The people of Alliance, Ohio
   (a) think that Everett was a bullfighter.
   (b) are poor drivers.
   (c) have praised Everett's work.
   (d) have voted Everett the "Traffic Cop of the Year."
4. Everett wanted to be a traffic cop because
   (a) he enjoyed his first job at an intersection.
   (b) he studied how to direct traffic.
   (c) he was tired of working in the factory.
   (d) the job pays very well.

5. In the story, Everett's work is compared to the work of

(a) a truck driver.

(b) a road builder.

(c) a bullfighter.

(d) a factory worker.

REACHING OUT

1. When Charles Everett finished work on his first job as a traffic cop, he was *not*

(a) angry.

(b) tired.

(c) in need of a shower.

(d) willing to do it again.

2. Everett could best be described as

(a) brave.

(b) kind.

(c) funny.

(d) energetic.

PUTTING THE PIECES TOGETHER

Below is a title for each of the seven paragraphs in the story. Put these titles in the order in which the paragraphs appeared in the story. The first one is done for you.

1. A Truck Driver's Opinion About Charles Everett

2. How Patrolman Everett Runs An Intersection

3. His First Traffic Job

4. Why Charles Everett Is Popular

5. Charles Everett Is Like a Bullfighter
6. Everett's Feelings About His First Traffic Job
7. Alliance, Ohio's Dancing Cop—Paragraph 1

GETTING THE PICTURE

Pick out the words in the second column that will correctly finish the picture started in the first column. The correct answer for the first one is c. "The traffic . . . kept getting thicker and thicker."

A	B
1. The traffic	(a) twists, dips and bends as if he were dancing.
2. Tar	
3. Charles Everett	(b) became soft under the broiling sun.
4. White gloves	
5. Road crews	(c) kept getting thicker and thicker.
	(d) were using water to cool the tar.
	(e) spin zigzag patterns.

IMPROVING YOUR VOCABULARY

In the first column below and on the next page are the ten words in italics from the story. Pick out the best "story" meaning of each of these words.

1. *fearless* fighter   (a) weak; (b) brave; (c) strong

2. *graceful* dancer   (a) thankful; (b) beautiful in movement; (c) strange

220

3. *enthusiasm* for a job — (a) jealousy; (b) high interest; (c) anger
4. keep traffic *flowing* — (a) working; (b) playing; (c) moving
5. entire *community* — (a) meeting; (b) city; (c) people of a town
6. run an *intersection* — (a) traffic corner; (b) traffic light; (c) highway
7. zigzag *patterns* — (a) dresses; (b) designs; (c) puzzles
8. *practical* way — (a) proud; (b) useless; (c) useful
9. a *huge* truck — (a) filled; (b) very large; (c) closed
10. a big *rig* — (a) truck; (b) bus; (c) road

WORD BUILDING

The word *unusual* from the story above means *not usual*. As you learned in Chapter 2, the prefix *un* often means *not*.

To Do: Match the meaning in column B to the proper *un* word in column A.

A	B
1. an *unkind* person	(a) not friendly
2. *unwilling* to help	(b) not fair
3. an *unfair* player	(c) not hurt
4. an *unfriendly* dog	(d) not willing
5. escaped *unhurt*	(e) not kind

A Little Harder: The prefix *un* has another meaning. Sometimes it means *to do the opposite.* For example, *untie* does not mean *not tie* but *to do the opposite of tie.*

For the word in italics in each sentence below, write NOT if the prefix *un* means *not;* write OPPOSITE if the *un* means *to do the opposite.*

1. My friend has to *undress* because we threw him in the lake with his clothes on.
2. The boss was away for two weeks and his mail was *unopened.*
3. The cook *uncovered* the pot to let the food cool.
4. Because of bad weather, our friends had an *unpleasant* vacation.
5. If your new mailing address is *unknown* to the post office, you will not receive your mail.
6. By *unfolding* the tablecloth, we will know whether it will fit the table.
7. The jeweler has to *unwind* our grandfather's clock.
8. Since my brother was ill, he left his homework *unfinished.*
9. We were *unhappy* when our trip was called off.
10. Seventy miles an hour is an *unsafe* speed.

EXPRESSING YOURSELF

1. Policemen have to perform many jobs. List five jobs that policemen have to do. Tell which jobs seem easy and which seem difficult to you. Which are safe, and which are dangerous?

2. When a person becomes a member of the police force, he must be available for any emergency —even if he is not on duty. Do you think this rule is a good one? Why?
3. Tell of a policeman you know or have heard about who has earned the respect of the people in your community. Why do the people like him?
4. Write a paragraph telling about some person you know who enjoys his job, just as Patrolman Charles Everett does.

30. THE MUSICAL WIZARD

SUCCESS COMES FROM A COMBINATION OF LUCK, NATURAL ABILITY AND HARD WORK.

WHICH OF THE THREE WAS MOST IMPORTANT TO ROLAND KIRK'S SUCCESS?

When Roland Kirk was fifteen years old, he dreamed one night he was playing three musical instruments — all at the same time. He made his dream come true. Today he is a *brilliant* musician with a *talent* so real few people can believe it.

When he blows one horn (for example, the tenor saxophone), he is the equal of any musician around today. When he blows three horns at the same time, he is truly out of this world.

Kirk is a one-man band, the master of forty-five musical instruments. Even more *amazing,* he has been blind since the age of two.

Kirk's regular instruments are the saxophone, the manzello and the stritch (both of which look like very long saxophones), and the flute. When he plays, he keeps the first three around his neck and the flute in the bell of his sax. Within arm's reach are also a one-foot siren, a cigar-shaped song flute and a humming box that he calls "The Evil Box."

In the middle of a flute *solo,* he may reach for the song flute and play a *duet,* using both his nose and his mouth. This is impossible for most musicians, but Kirk, who has made a study of breath

225

control, can do it. He has learned to use his lungs to *capacity* and to store air in his cheeks.

Kirk discovered the magic of music as a child in Columbus, Ohio. "When I was six," he *recalled,* "I tried to play music with a water hose. Later, I learned to play the bugle at a summer camp where my mother and father were *counselors.* After that, I took up the trumpet."

Kirk is world-famous, already rated among the giants of jazz. An English jazz musician, who can play three instruments — but only one at a time — said after hearing Kirk play, "He is just unbelievable. Did you know that when he *relaxes* he listens to the radio, record-player and television all at once?"

This blind musical *genius,* master of forty-five instruments, is — amazingly — self-taught.

— EBONY

CHECK YOUR UNDERSTANDING

1. Another title that would best explain the main idea of this story is:
   (a) One-Man Bands
   (b) Teaching Yourself Music
   (c) Blind Since the Age of Two
   (d) An Amazing Musician
2. Roland Kirk is amazing because he
   (a) made his dream come true.
   (b) can play three horns at the same time.
   (c) tried to play music with a water hose.
   (d) played the bugle at a summer camp.

3. Kirk
   (a) is not really a good musician.
   (b) is the master of forty-five instruments.
   (c) was born in England.
   (d) became famous at the age of fifteen.
4. Of these instruments, the one Kirk learned to play first was the
   (a) saxophone.
   (b) trumpet.
   (c) flute.
   (d) manzello.
5. When Roland Kirk was fifteen, he
   (a) could play three instruments at once.
   (b) was a counselor at a summer camp.
   (c) had a dream he was playing three instruments at the same time.
   (d) started taking music lessons.

REACHING OUT

When he plays, Kirk does *not* keep around his neck
   (a) the flute.
   (b) the manzello.
   (c) the saxophone.
   (d) the stritch.

PUTTING THE PIECES TOGETHER

On the next page is a title for each of the eight paragraphs in this story. Put these titles in the order

in which the paragraphs appeared in the story. The
first one is done for you.

1. A Blind One-Man Band
2. Kirk Plays a Duet
3. Great With One Horn or Three
4. A Self-Taught Musician
5. Kirk's Early Musical Interests
6. Roland Kirk's Dream—Paragraph 1
7. The Instruments Kirk Uses
8. The Opinion of an English Musician

IMPROVING YOUR VOCABULARY

In the first column below and on the next page
are the ten words in italics from the story. Pick out
the best "story" meaning of each of these words.

1. *brilliant* musician   (a) old; (b) very able; (c) real

2. real *talent*   (a) musical instrument; (b) dream; (c) ability

3. *amazing* man   (a) talented; (b) very surprising; (c) heart-breaking

4. flute *solo*   (a) music for one instrument; (b) song; (c) presentation to an audience

5. play a *duet*   (a) flute song; (b) music for one instrument; (c) music for two instruments

6. use to *capacity*   (a) great care; (b) con-

228

trol; (c) all that can be
contained

7. he *recalled* (a) remembered; (b)
spoke slowly; (c) called
loudly

8. camp *counselors* (a) musicians; (b) advisers; (c) caretakers

9. he *relaxes* (a) rests from work; (b)
works; (c) plays music

10. musical *genius* (a) person with very
great natural ability; (b)
person who teaches him-
self music; (c) person
who makes a great deal
of money

WORD BUILDING

The word *television* is used in the story above.
We all know what the word means, but how did it
get its meaning? The prefix *tele* means *from a distance,* the stem *vis* means *seeing,* and the suffix *sion*
means *a means of.* So *television* is a *means of seeing from a distance.*

Usually, *vis* or *vid* in a word means *see* or
seeing.

Example: The word *visit* means *go to see.*

To Do: Match the meaning in column B to
the proper *vis* or *vid* word in column A.

A **B**

1. *visible* view (a) sense of sight

2. *visitor* arrives   (b) see to the future;
3. *provide* for the trip   prepare
4. keen *vision*   (c) able to be seen
5. *visualize* a wild horse   (d) to "see" in the
     mind
     (e) person who has
     come to see

More: The prefix *tele* in a word means *from a distance* or *from afar*. For example, a *telephoto* camera lens is one that produces a large picture of a *distant* object.

Match the meaning in column B to the proper *tele* word in column A.

A	B
1. work the *telegraph*	(a) television broadcast
2. answer the *telephone*	(b) instrument for making distant objects look nearer and larger
3. look through the *telescope*	
4. received a *telegram*	(c) instrument for sending speech from a distance
5. an unclear *telecast*	(d) instrument for sending messages from a distance
	(e) message sent by a telegraph

EXPRESSING YOURSELF

1. What roles did natural ability and hard work play in Roland Kirk's success?

2. Do you think Kirk would have become as great a musician if he had *not* been blind? Explain your answer.
3. Tell of someone you know or heard about who has unusual ability. How did he develop it?
4. Tell about your experiences with music.
5. Write a paragraph telling of a musician or entertainer whom you enjoy and admire.

REVIEW OF LESSONS 26-30

IMPROVING YOUR VOCABULARY

Choose the correct meaning of the words below. (The number in parentheses after each word
tells you which lesson the word first appeared in.)

1. amazing (30)   (a) funny; (b) very surprising; (c) tall

2. blazing (27)   (a) dying; (b) sharp; (c)
flaming

3. brilliant (30)   (a) very poor; (b) very
fast; (c) very able

4. capacity (30)   (a) largest amount that
can be contained; (b) not
full; (c) large town

5. community (29)   (a) people of an area or
a town; (b) world; (c)
voters

232

6. counselors (30)   (a) people who add; (b) prisoners; (c) advisers

7. crushes (26)   (a) drinks; (b) breaks into small pieces; (c) carries

8. cure (26)   (a) cut open; (b) make well; (c) close down

9. duet (30)   (a) music for two instruments; (b) money owed; (c) an air hole

10. emotional (26)   (a) able to move; (b) having strong feelings; (c) unable to move

11. enthusiasm (29)   (a) low interest; (b) pride; (c) high interest

12. fearless (29)   (a) brave; (b) free; (c) afraid

13. fever (26)   (a) high body temperature; (b) spring; (c) low body temperature

14. flowing (29)   (a) moving; (b) having flowers; (c) making air

15. freshly (28)   (a) old; (b) nicely; (c) newly

16. gap (27)   (a) look at; (b) space; (c) stick

17. genius (30)   (a) person who makes magic; (b) ghost; (c) person with great natural ability

18. graceful (29)   (a) thankful; (b) beautiful in movement; (c) full of grass

19. grenade (28)   (a) small bomb; (b) fruit; (c) rifle

233

20. height (27)   (a) how wide something is; (b) how heavy something is; (c) how tall something is

21. huge (29)   (a) very large; (b) to hold tightly; (c) very small

22. important (26)   (a) fake; (b) valuable or worth notice; (c) heavy

23. instinct (28)   (a) natural feeling; (b) not clean; (c) smell

24. intersection (29)   (a) part; (b) traffic corner; (c) turn

25. method (26)   (a) way of doing things; (b) story; (c) machine

26. mixture (26)   (a) oil; (b) lamp; (c) that which has been stirred

27. motioning (27)   (a) pulling; (b) pushing; (c) showing what you mean

28. patrol (28)   (a) group of soldiers going the rounds; (b) trick; (c) something used to jump from an airplane

29. patterns (29)   (a) tapping; (b) designs; (c) dresses

30. plunged (28)   (a) dived; (b) danced; (c) swam

31. power (26)   (a) spill; (b) loud noise; (c) might

32. practical (29)   (a) drill; (b) useful; (c) good

33. recalled (30)   (a) remembered; (b) forgot; (c) whistled

34. relaxes (30) (a) rests from work; (b) stretches; (c) gets tired

35. rig (29) (a) fruit; (b) shovel; (c) truck

36. risked (27) (a) took a dangerous chance; (b) cleaned; (c) raced

37. separated (27) (a) put together; (b) taken apart; (c) nearby

38. shrieks (28) (a) trembles; (b) Arab people; (c) sharp, loud sounds

39. skidded (28) (a) stopped; (b) slid sideways; (c) skated

40. solo (30) (a) game; (b) music for one instrument; (c) loose

41. stirs (26) (a) steps; (b) mixes; (c) begins

42. submerge (28) (a) boat; (b) float; (c) sink

43. success (27) (a) poor results; (b) good results; (c) gravy

44. supported (27) (a) held up; (b) held down; (c) let go

45. suppose (26) (a) imagine; (b) stocking; (c) offer to marry

46. survived (28) (a) died; (b) got away; (c) stayed alive

47. talent (30) (a) musical instrument; (b) very tall; (c) ability

48. threatened (27) (a) placed into danger; (b) offered; (c) cooked

49. unconscious (27) (a) painful; (b) unable to feel; (c) unable to sleep

50. widow (28) (a) opening in the wall; (b) woman whose husband is dead; (c) husband whose wife is dead

---

WORD-BUILDING PARTS

Match the meaning in column B to the proper word-building part in column A.

A	B
1. *vis* (30)	(a) not; to do the opposite
2. *ure* (26)	(b) the result of an act
3. *mot, mov* (27)	(c) under
4. *sub* (28)	(d) from afar
5. *tele* (30)	(e) see or seeing
6. *un* (29)	(f) move

WORD BUILDING

Listed below are several of the words you "built up" in the last five lessons. Choose the correct meaning of each.

1. exposure (26) (a) result of uncovering; (b) result of posing; (c) result of telling

2. pleasure (26) (a) result of working; (b) result of fixing; (c) result of making happy

3. pressure (26) (a) result of rushing; (b) result of pressing; (c) result of being sure

4. promote (27)   (a) to move forward; (b) to move backward; (c) to move sideways

5. provide (30)   (a) prepare; (b) make angry; (c) make safe

6. motive (27)   (a) machine; (b) saying; (c) thought or feeling that makes someone do something

7. motor (27)   (a) boat; (b) engine that makes a machine go; (c) robot

8. movable (27)   (a) able to move; (b) unable to move; (c) able to see a picture

9. movies (27)   (a) sounds that are loud; (b) pictures that move quickly; (c) slide

10. seizure (26)   (a) result of freeing; (b) result of eating; (c) result of taking by force

11. signature (26)   (a) result of signing a name; (b) making a sign; (c) singing a song

12. submarine (28)   (a) underwater balloon; (b) underwater boat; (c) ocean liner

13. to submit (28)   (a) to fight; (b) to dare; (c) to give in

14. subsoil (28)   (a) just under the top layer of earth; (b) to take away; (c) grass

15. subtitle (28)   (a) paragraph; (b) sentence; (c) second or additional title

16. subway (28)   (a) underground train; (b) bus; (c) ski lift

17. telecast (30)   (a) actor; (b) movie; (c) television broadcast

18. telegram (30)   (a) phone call; (b) message sent by telegraph; (c) code

19. telegraph (30)   (a) instrument for sending speech from far away; (b) instrument for sending pictures; (c) instrument for sending messages a long way

20. telephone (30)   (a) instrument for sending speech from far away; (b) instrument for making distant objects look near; (c) instrument for sending pictures

21. telescope (30)   (a) instrument for sending messages from a long distance; (b) instrument for making distant objects look nearer and larger; (c) instrument for sending speech a long distance

22. unfair (29)   (a) not fair; (b) fair; (c) cheap

23. unfriendly (29)   (a) very friendly; (b) not friendly; (c) not a cousin

24. unhurt (29)   (a) sad; (b) not hurt; (c) hurt

25. unkind (29)   (a) kind; (b) not the same; (c) not kind

26. unwilling (29)   (a) not wanting; (b) not

27. visible (30)   working; (c) not willing (a) able to leave; (b) able to be seen; (c) able to hold

28. vision (30)   (a) sense of touch; (b) sense of smell; (c) sense of sight

29. visitor (30)   (a) person who drives; (b) person who hides; (c) person who comes to "see" or call on

30. visualize (30)   (a) to "see" in the mind; (b) having to do with visiting; (c) having to do with touch

A Little Harder: Match the meaning in column B to the proper word in column A.

A	B
1. capture (26)	(a) something put in place to stay
2. fixture (26)	
3. fracture (26)	(b) not as good as expected
4. leisure (26)	
5. moisture (26)	(c) catch
6. subdivide (28)	(d) to defeat
7. subdue (28)	(e) to separate into smaller parts
8. substandard (28)	
9. substance (28)	(f) break
10. substitute (28)	(g) the stuff of which something is made
	(h) free time
	(i) to take the place of something
	(j) slight wetness

WRAPPING IT UP: A REVIEW OF LESSONS 16-30

a child sho..., not obey his parents?

Priscilla Brown is a very good child. She is only six years old but is responsible nd obedient. She takes excel-ent care of her four younger -rothers and never disobeys er mother. Since yesterday, owever, Mrs. Mary Brown, er mother, probably thinks he is a little too obedient.

The Browns live in the hird floor of an apartment ouse in Brooklyn. Roderick Thompson, four years old, ives in an adjoining apart-nent. At 9 A.M. yesterday, Roderick noticed smoke curl-ng from under the Browns' loor. He called his mother, Mrs. Sophie Thompson, who ang the doorbell and pounded n the door until Priscilla re-lied.

"Who's that?" the girl alled through the locked loor.

"This is Mrs. Thompson. Open the door, honey." Mrs. Thompson was careful not to darm the child.

"No. My mommy says I mustn't open the door to any-ody."

"But Priscilla, I think here's a fire in your house."

...cess to ...e roof and ...n to go below the height of the flames. He could not do so while carrying the dead-weight of the helpless 115-pound woman.

Then he saw another fire-man, Mike Mays, motioning to him with his arms held out. Mays was on the roof of the next building, which was level with the fire escape. A space of only four feet separated the two buildings, but there was a fifty-foot drop to the ground. Lane tried to pass Mrs. Rogers over to Mays, but the gap was too wide.

Then the two men decided that the only chance to save the woman was to try some-thing very dangerous. Lane reached back and threw Mrs. Rogers across the space be-tween the buildings. For a moment the woman was not supported above the ground. Then Mays caught her by the neck and shoulders, and pulled her safely onto the roof. Mrs. Rogers was uninjured.

Lane then climbed to the roof of the burning building, went down another fire escape and back to fighting the fire

—NEWSDAY
(Long Island, N.Y.)

Mosquitoes

---

one night ... musical instrumes ... the same time. He made dream come true. Today he a brilliant musician with a ta ent so real few people can b lieve it.

When he blows one ho: (for example, the tenor sax phone), he is the equal of ar musician around today. Wh be blows three horns at t same time, he is truly out this world.

Kirk is a one-man band, t master of forty-five music instruments. Even more ama ing, he has been blind sin the age of two.

Kirk's regular instrumes are the saxophone, the ma zello and the stritch (both which look like very long sa ophones), and the flute. Wh he plays, he keeps the fi three around his neck and t flute in the bell of his sa Within arm's reach are also one-foot siren, a cigar-shap song flute---and a humml box that he calls "The E Box."

In the middle of the fl solo, he may reach for song flute and play a du using both his nose and mouth. This is impossible most musicians, but Kirk, w has made a study of bre: control, can do it. He I learned to use his lungs capacity and to store air in cheeks.

Kirk discovered the ma

IMPROVING YOUR VOCABULARY

Here is a review of the words you learned in the last fifteen lessons. Choose the correct meaning of each word.

1. accept   (a) leave out; (b) take; (c) give

2. amazing   (a) tricky; (b) large; (c) wonderful

3. appointment   (a) being sharp; (b) naming to a job; (c) talking aloud

4. attract   (a) take away; (b) listen carefully; (c) draw to oneself

5. avoid   (a) empty; (b) keep away from; (c) meet with

6. certain   (a) some; (b) none; (c) all

7. citizenship   (a) being a member of a city; (b) being a member of the army; (c) being a member of a country

8. command   (a) calm; (b) take charge; (c) make angry

9. community   (a) a park; (b) the police; (c) the people of an area

10. contest   (a) trial of skill; (b) prize; (c) school test

11. counselors   (a) leaders; (b) advisers; (c) losers

12. cure   (a) make sick; (b) make old; (c) make well

13. defend	(a) hurt badly; (b) keep from harm; (c) force
14. describe	(a) tell in words how something looks; (b) clean; (c) write neatly
15. disease	(a) illness; (b) sleep; (c) health
16. emotional	(a) strong; (b) having strong feelings; (c) being fast
17. exactly	(a) late; (b) on time; (c) without any error
18. exciting	(a) different; (b) only; (c) thrilling
19. experience	(a) a fast train; (b) unusual happening; (c) very good
20. experts	(a) people who care; (b) people who know a lot about some special subject; (c) people who dream
21. explained	(a) told why; (b) spoke loudly; (c) begged
22. fame	(a) being hungry; (b) being fat; (c) being well-known
23. fashions	(a) designs; (b) pants; (c) clothing styles
24. frequently	(a) once in a while; (b) all the time; (c) often
25. genius	(a) ghost; (b) player; (c) person with great natural ability
26. graceful	(a) thankful; (b) beautiful in movement; (c) slow
27. harmless	(a) safe; (b) painful; (c) painless

28. height   (a) how fat someone is; (b) how old someone is; (c) how tall someone is

29. human   (a) living creature; (b) person; (c) person with great natural ability

30. inject   (a) pull out; (b) force into; (c) press down

31. instinct   (a) thinking about; (b) smelling; (c) feeling to act

32. license   (a) insect; (b) glass; (c) permit

33. method   (a) way of feeling; (b) way of driving; (c) way of doing things

34. minor   (a) safe; (b) important; (c) not serious

35. modern   (a) normal; (b) down-to-earth; (c) up-to-date

36. motorist   (a) driver; (b) car repairman; (c) walker

37. nations   (a) planets; (b) countries; (c) cities

38. opportunity   (a) chance; (b) business; (c) luck

39. power   (a) might; (b) light; (c) work

40. practical   (a) extra; (b) skillful; (c) useful

41. protect   (a) keep safe; (b) keep near; (c) keep on

42. relaxes   (a) runs; (b) rests; (c) sits

43. replied   (a) lied again; (b) filled; (c) answered

44. **responsible** (a) able to answer; (b) able to be trusted; (c) able to help

45. **risked** (a) brushed; (b) took a dangerous chance; (c) searched

46. **saliva** (a) liquid in the mouth; (b) sugar; (c) hungry

47. **scholarship** (a) ship; (b) student; (c) free education

48. **section** (a) stick on; (b) part; (c) plan

49. **sketch** (a) rough drawing; (b) small boat; (c) itch

50. **solo** (a) music for two voices; (b) music for one instrument; (c) music for three voices

51. **spare** (a) one; (b) fight; (c) extra

52. **suppose** (a) enjoy; (b) act; (c) imagine

53. **swollen** (a) larger than usual; (b) smaller than usual; (c) sneeze

54. **talent** (a) tall; (b) ability; (c) powder

55. **tense** (a) nervous; (b) feeling; (c) thick

56. **threatened** (a) made sweet; (b) made thick; (c) placed into danger

57. **traveling** (a) moving about; (b) following; (c) selling

58. **type** (a) way; (b) kind; (c) time

59. **universe** (a) world; (b) nation; (c) city

60. **wealthy** (a) poor; (b) rich; (c) in good health

WORD BUILDING

Match the meaning in column B to the proper word-building part in column A.

A	**B**
1. *scrib, scrip*	(a) see or seeing
2. *mot, mov*	(b) from afar
3. *ship*	(c) under
4. *inter*	(d) between, among, with one another
5. *sub*	
6. *per*	(e) able to be
7. *able, ible*	(f) the result of an act
8. *tele*	(g) write
9. *vis, vid*	(h) through or very
10. *ject*	(i) move
	(j) throw

A Little Harder: Match the meaning in column B to the proper word in column A.

A	**B**
1. interrupt	(a) the result of liking another person
2. interview	
3. subdue	(b) defeat
4. friendship	(c) let, allow
5. permit	(d) able to be moved
6. rejected	(e) thought or feeling that makes someone do something
7. pressure	
8. motive	
9. movable	(f) turned down or refused
10. submarine	(g) break in on
	(h) ship that can travel underwater
	(i) the result of pressing
	(j) visit and talk with